WORKING
WITH
WILDLIFE

WORKING WITH WILDLIFE

A Guide to Careers in the Animal World

by
Thane Maynard

Foreword by Jane Goodall

FRANKLIN WATTS
A Division of Grolier Publishing
New York   London   Hong Kong   Sydney
Danbury, Connecticut

This book is dedicated to three people who helped me on my own journey working with wildlife:

Fleet Peeples — the legendary Florida naturalist, who got me started so long ago

Tom Harblin — my college mentor and role model, who showed me that life and work can be rewarding

Bill Stapp — scholar-athlete and the father of environmental education, who always knew how to pull people together.

—T.M.

Frontis: A biologist prepares to release a rehabilitated red-tailed hawk.

Interior design by Molly Heron
Photographs ©: Alexis Rockman: 107; Andy Baker: 24, 43, 60, 122; Anne Savage: 22, 38 bottom, 80 top; Bat Conservation International, Inc.: 39 bottom; Berman: 92; Cheetah Conservation Fund: 29, 96, 124; Cincinnati Zoo: 79 top (Ron Austing), 20, 52, 58 (Debbie Lentz), 13, 21, 25, 34 top, 40 bottom, 73 top, 111, 113; Columbus Zoo: 70, 74 top (Becky Rose); Connie Speight: 23; Dave Jenike: 71, 114; E. G. Photo: 32, 66 bottom; George Uetz: 67; Jackie Belwood: 101; Jane Goodall Institute: 61; Jonquil LeMaster: 104; Kathleen Stewart: cover top left, 33, 36 bottom, 85, 87, 95, 105, 109, 110; Kike Arnal: 64; Malcolm Wilson: 12; Mark Plotkin: 97; Mary Lou Drake: 50; Michael P. Moore: 47, 69, 77 top, 78, 79 bottom, 94, 120; National Geographic Image Collection: 6 (Baron Hugo Van Lawick); Oregon Zoo: 49; Rich Block: 27 (Kansas City Zoo), cover top right, cover bottom left, 34 bottom, 35, 36 top, 42, 63; Roger Tory Peterson Institute: 80 bottom; Ron Austing: 2, 76 bottom, 83, 84, 108; Russ Kinne: 106; S. David Jenike: 37 bottom; San Diego Zoo: 44; Snow Leopard Trust: 98; Stan Rullman: 37 top (Brian Peck), 41, 75 bottom, 76 top, 77 bottom; Thane Maynard: 38 top, 40 top, 45, 66 top, 88, 93, 99, 119; USFWS: 75 top (M. Alan Jenkins); Wildlife Conservation Society: 14, 15, 68; William B. Stapp: 82; William R. Konstant: 48; World Wildlife Fund Collection: 73 bottom (Tim Rautert), 74 bottom (Susan Walker), cover bottom right, 39 top; Zoological Society of San Diego: 54 (Ron Gordon Garrison).

Visit Franklin Watts on the Internet at:
http://publishing.grolier.com

Library of Congress Cataloging-in-Publication Data
Maynard, Thane.
    Working with Wildlife: a guide to careers in the animal world / by Thane Maynard: with a foreword by Jane Goodall.
        p.   cm.
    Includes bibliographical references (p.   ) and index.
    Summary: A detailed survey of the career fields open to those who wish to work with wildlife, including veterinary medicine, zoo and aquarium careers, research, education, conservation, and more.
        ISBN 0–531–11538–0 (lib. bdg.)   0-531-16415-2 (pbk)
    1. Animal specialists—Vocational guidance—Juvenile literature. 2. Animal culture—Vocational guidance—Juvenile literature.
[1. Animal specialists—Vocational guidance. 2. Vocational guidance. 3. Occupations.]   I. Title.
SF80.M39   1999
636'.0023—dc21   99–12300
                                                                           CIP

CONTENTS

FOREWORD
by
Jane Goodall

I first wanted to go to Africa, live with animals, and write books about them when I was about ten years old. I had read about Doctor Dolittle, the English doctor who was taught to speak the languages of all animals by his parrot, Polynesia. And then I found the books of Edgar Rice Burroughs about Tarzan of the Apes. I fell in love with my mental image of the Lord of the Jungle—and was very jealous of his wife, Jane. (And thought I'd have been a much better mate for him myself!)

When I first began my chimpanzee study in 1960, it was not considered "scientific" to give names to one's study animals. Numbers were more appropriate. Nor should I have described the chimpanzees' personalities, minds, or emotions. Those were qualities that could only be applied to humans. Fortunately, although at that time I had not been to college and had no degree, I had had a truly wonderful teacher all through my childhood: my dog, Rusty. He taught me so much about an animal's personality and ability to reason and feel emotions like happiness, sadness, crossness, and so on. I was confident that Rusty had taught me well. Now *science* teaches the same lessons that Rusty taught!

I got my Ph.D. much later—after spending some years in the field. I learned how to write in a way acceptable to scientists, but without compromising my absolute belief in the personality, rationality, and feelings of animals—certainly all vertebrate animals. This conviction keeps me focused on working toward a more humane and compassionate way of treating animals—not only wild animals, but also those with whom we share our lives: pets, farm animals, and so on.

There are so many ways in which we can help animals. The books I have written for the general public have had far more impact than my scientific papers, but the science was important as it taught me self-discipline and gave me credibility. Today we need more and more talented young people, educated in a variety of disciplines, in order to conserve the environment and its wild creatures. At Gombe, in Tanzania, we constantly need the advice and help of veterinarians. We need ecologists and population biologists and geneticists, as well as ethologists.

People with training in these fields are needed everywhere. And we need those with the ability to bring the problems of conservation to the hearts and minds of the general public—journalists, science writers, artists, singers. Of special importance are teachers: teachers of all grades—from preschool to university.

We need people who know about and care about and love animals, people with energy and dedication and wisdom. We need them in our zoos, national parks and preserves, in the farming world, in city planning, and in wilderness areas around the world. We need people in every walk of life who understand our relationship with the rest of the animal kingdom.

When I first dreamed of living with animals in Africa, people laughed. It was half a century ago. Africa was known as the "Dark Continent." It was far, far away, wild and primitive and savage. You went there by boat. Moreover, my family didn't have much money—enough for food and some clothes, but not enough for a bicycle, let alone a car.

"Dream of something you can actually achieve," people said. Except for my mother. Her message was different: "If you really want something and work hard and take advantage of opportunities and never give up, you will find a way." Well, I did! And so can you. If you have a dream of working with, of helping animals and their world, don't let anyone tell you it is impossible. Just remember my mother's advice—it is mine: "Follow your dream."

—Jane Goodall

YOU CAN DO ANYTHING— BUT YOU CANNOT DO EVERYTHING

Because I do what I do for a living—working as the education director of the Cincinnati Zoo—my telephone rings off the hook every day with calls from people of all ages who want to work with animals: kids who want to grow up to be veterinarians, college students who want to travel to the tropical rain forests, and people from all over the country who want to help save wildlife. A few even say that they are going to quit their day jobs and become the next Jane Goodall!

For all of them I have genuine good news: working with wildlife is a growth industry. There are more jobs today than ever before that involve biology, wildlife, and wild areas, and the future looks even more challenging. The more crowded and developed Earth becomes, the more work it will take to protect life on Earth. And there is far more that we do not know than there is that we do know, so there is plenty of work for researchers. All it takes to get into these fields is dedication and hard work. So get to it!

This book is an introduction to careers and opportunities for working with animals. I am not going to talk about jobs such as

THANE MAYNARD   *Zoo Educator*

*T*hane Maynard is director of education at the Cincinnati Zoo and Botanical Garden. He is writer and host of the National Public Radio daily feature "The 90-Second Naturalist" and "Thane Maynard's Wild World," a daily television news feature that celebrates the wonders of nature and biodiversity. He got his start working with wildlife in central Florida in the days before air conditioning and affluence swept over the "Sunshine State." Starting off as a volunteer with the Florida Audubon Society while going to college, and later working as an intern for the Smithsonian Institution, he gained enough interest and experience to go on to graduate school at the University of Michigan's School of Natural Resources. Since that time he has been keenly interested in reaching the general public about the wonders of nature and the importance of protecting wildlife and wild places.

Working with wildlife is a growth industry, especially in the zoo business. Janet Ramsey is an animal trainer who works with cheetahs and other exotic animals.

animal groomer, Seeing Eye-dog trainer, kennel operator, or others that involve work with domesticated animals. Here you will find more about work with nondomesticated, or exotic, animals.

Some future wildlife-worker hopefuls don't call, they just stop by. Students and recent graduates drop by my office at the zoo on a regular basis, to talk about working with wildlife. By the time they get to me, most of them are already convinced that they want to be veterinarians, or zookeepers, or animal trainers. The trouble is that they don't have a clue about how to get started.

Getting started can be more complicated than it seems. Some people appear to be so bright and hard-driving that it's easy to assume that they always know where they're going. They seem to fit in immediately and start solving problems. It is important to remember, though, that it only *seems* as if other people have a better idea of what they're doing and where they're heading.

Everybody is guessing a lot of the time. The important thing is to keep trying.

Do not wait until you win the lottery to do what you want to do. You would be amazed at how many well-educated people who

Where do you want to go? How about to the snow-covered peaks of Alaska to study Arctic birds?

14

have all the options in the world open to them waste their time waiting for something to happen. Some say that they always wanted to be field biologists, but they were waiting for the right moment. Others had hoped to go back to school someday to get an advanced degree so they would be prepared to do the work they had always dreamed of. But as the old saying tells us, "Life is what happens to you while you're making other plans." Get up and get going. Do not wait for "something" to happen to get started.

The worst thing that would-be wildlife workers can say to me when I ask what they most want to do, is that they wish they could win the lottery so that they would then have the freedom to pursue their dreams. The great news is that they are completely wrong! I have met a few people who have won the lottery

What do you want to do? How about rescuing a white-lipped peccary in the steamy tropics?

The Nonconcentric Circles Theory of Wildlife Careers

Some people are lucky. They want to do just one thing, and they are good enough at that one thing to make a living at it. But most of us have careers that require lots of different skills. My own career has been like a Swiss Army knife, with lots of different jobs and opportunities and challenges along the way. And like that little, utilitarian red knife, I have needed to be able to do more than just one thing. Most of the time I have had to do two or more things at the same time.

You can take on various jobs that are totally unrelated—say, being a college biology professor and a chef. That may work for you. But you will gain more from your work if your different skills and jobs overlap. For instance, if you are a college biology professor but also write journal articles and books about natural history and conduct field research in the summer with your graduate students, you can build on the strengths of your overlapping skills. (It's also a good idea to develop as many skills as possible.)

and were instantly rendered millionaires who would "not have to work another day in their lives." The trouble is, as ecologists teach us, "There's no such thing as a free lunch." Folks who experience incredible windfalls, like winning millions of dollars, often are so occupied with managing the changes all that money made to their lives, that they have neither the time nor the energy to figure out what else it is they want to do anyway.

Besides, the simple fact that you are holding this book in your hands means that you've already won the *evolutionary* lottery. It took billions of years of evolution just for humans to appear on the scene a few million years ago. Since that time we people have changed the environment around us dramatically, but we have not changed all that much ourselves. There is one thing for certain, though—when your mom and dad got together and created you, *that* was the real lottery worth winning. You are one in 6 billion (the current human population on Earth), and there is no other like you.

The important thing to remember is what it is you'd really like to do—because you *can* do anything! But remember, it's essential to focus your energies because, while you *can* do anything, you *can't* do everything!

Once you've got your heart set on the things you most want to do with your life, make a list. I know it sounds a little compul-

Top Books for Future Naturalists

Naturalist by Edward O. Wilson
A Sand County Almanac by Aldo Leopold
The Year of the Gorilla by George Schaller
Through a Window by Jane Goodall
Megadiversity by Russ Mittermeier
My Family and Other Animals by Gerald Durell
The Primary Source by Norman Myers
Tales of a Shaman's Apprentice by Mark Plotkin

Top Magazines for Future Naturalists

National Geographic
Natural History
Wildlife Conservation
National Wildlife
International Wildlife
Outside
Audubon

sive, but the value of the list is that it will help you figure out what your next steps are. And, just as when you are climbing a steep mountain, you need to keep going.

For example, if what you really want to do is write books about wildlife, take every chance that you get to write: in school and during summers, on planes or buses, at the beach, in a journal or at your computer. And it's just as important for you to read as much as you can, and to get as much life experience as possible, so that you'll have something to write about.

So set your goals, get a compass, get some miles under your hiking boots, and go whip the world. You will know you're getting it done when people start to ask you how they can get a job like yours.

one
VETERINARY MEDICINE

For those who deal with animals we ask a heart of compassion and gentle hands and kindly words.
Albert Schweitzer

Without a doubt, the field I am most often asked about is veterinary medicine. This is partly because medicine, whether for human or non-human patients, has been an important field of work throughout history. We appreciate and trust the people we choose to take care of ourselves, our families, and our critters. But I think the primary reason that so many people want to be veterinarians "when they grow up" is that our first contacts with creatures are nearly always with our own pets. And the primary caregivers for our pets are the women and men at the vet's office.

Veterinary medicine is a rewarding and challenging field of work. It requires as much preparation and as much schooling as any wildlife career, so it is a good idea to acquire as much experience as possible in related work areas before committing to this career path. You want to be sure that your interest in the field will continue. For instance, if you take your family pets to a veterinarian, ask if you could spend part of a day helping at the office. As a volunteer you might get the chance to do everything from cleaning cages to holding animals during examinations. If

MARK CAMPBELL   *Zoo Veterinarian*

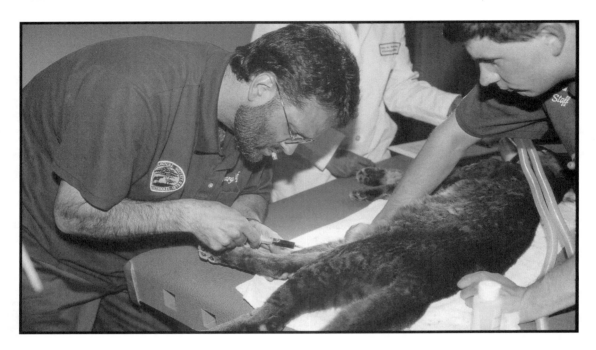

Dr. Mark Campbell has the hardest job at the zoo. Not just because he is responsible for the health of thousands of wild animals, but also because he works longer hours than anyone else there. "Doc," as he is known to everyone, is chief veterinarian at the Cincinnati Zoo and Botanical Garden. He is one of three vets on staff, but the ultimate responsibility for the well being of the collection rests with him.

Being a vet is challenging, particularly since the patients cannot tell you what hurts. With wild animals in a zoo, a veterinarian must rely on preventative medicine to insure the overall health of the collection. This strategy means that the vet must be involved in everything from the animals' diets to the keeping of detailed medical records on all the animals in the zoo. Doc depends directly on these records and the input of the animal keepers for information. The keepers work with the collection every day and know the animals best. Working together, the keepers and the veterinary staff insure the long-term success of the zoo.

you make yourself useful, they may ask you back. But no matter what happens, you will certainly gain a little experience in the real world of veterinary medicine.

Most vets work with small domestic animals—cats, dogs, and birds. Others have large-animal practices, specializing in horses or livestock. Other vets work with nondomesticated animals—called exotic animals. These exotic animal veterinarians most often gain practical, hands-on experience by working in zoos, aquariums, or wildlife rehabilitation centers after completing their formal schooling. This training system is similar to the internship and residency programs in human medicine. Some internships can be taken while still in vet school. Residencies, such as veterinary ophthalmology, are generally entered after graduation from veterinary medicine programs and last at least two years.

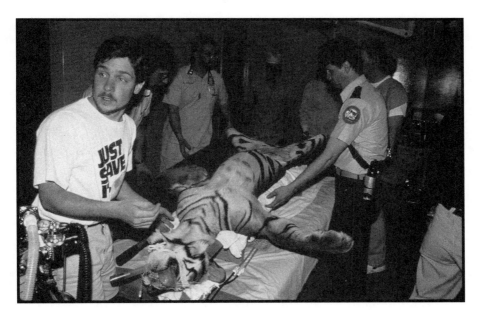

Zoo veterinarians and keepers monitor the health of an Indo-Chinese tiger before a reproductive physiology exam.

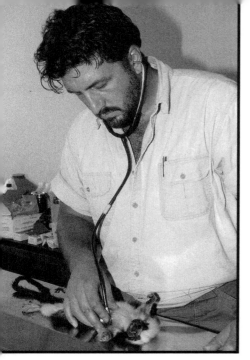

Veterinarian Evan Blumer conducts a physical examination on a cotton-top tamarin.

The two most common careers in exotic-animal veterinary medicine are those of the veterinarian and the veterinary technician (see page 26). These are the women and men responsible for the medical care of nondomesticated animals. They conduct routine preventive checkups on captive animals, perform surgery when necessary, and prescribe medicine and dietary changes to improve the animals' health. In addition, some vets and vet techs work with free-roaming animal populations in national parks and nature reserves around the world.

Exotic-animal veterinarians generally work either full time in a zoo or aquarium setting or in their own private practice. There has been tremendous expansion and improvement over the last twenty-five years in zoo and aquarium facilities and there are important advances in zoo and aquarium

A Note about Money

Wildlife careers are for people who love living things. Generally these are folks who would rather be outdoors than in an office and who care about the beauty of the sky and the natural world. Generally, jobs working with animals or careers that take you to wild places do not pay as much as, say, working in business or in high-tech fields. Most people in wildlife careers, if they stick with it and do a good job, earn about as much as schoolteachers. The pay is plenty to get along on, but you probably won't get rich in these fields. On the other hand, the many benefits include loving what you do and feeling that it is worthwhile, important work.

A vet performing a dental exam on an anesthetized African cheetah.

medicine all the time. Most zoo vets are extremely busy people, so it may not be possible to "shadow" or volunteer directly for them. But keep your eyes open for special programs offered at your nearest zoo or aquarium. Often the medical staff will give talks or seminars in which they explain their work—a great chance to hear firsthand what such work is like.

Zoo and aquarium veterinary programs share a great deal of information about the treatment of exotic animals. Through the use of the Internet, e-mail, scientific publications, and a program called **MEDARKS** (medical animal record keeping system), zoo veterinary personnel can consult with colleagues at other institutions more easily than ever before. Check out some of these resources to learn more about exotic-animal veterinary medicine. A good place to start is NetVet Veterinary Services, which can be found on the Web (www.netvet.wustl.edu/). With the Internet, you're not limited to your local zoo but can access information from most of the zoos,

Mr. Thane Maynard
Cincinnati Zoo & Botanical Garden
3400 Vine Street
Cincinnati, OH 45220

Dear Mr. Maynard:
I am a zoology major at the University
of Vermont in Burlington. I am most
interested in becoming a veterinarian.
What are your suggestions for where I
could study for this field?

Any help you could provide would be
greatly appreciated.

Sincerely yours,

Greg Schmeltzer

aquariums, and vet schools around the world.

Veterinarians in private practice generally treat domestic breeds, but may also treat exotic animals, such as tropical birds or reptiles. Private veterinarians are also frequently called upon by groups involved with wildlife rehabilitation to treat injured local wildlife. A successful veterinary practice can be lucrative, but vets who are on call to aid local

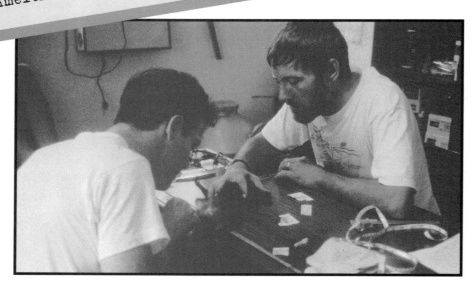

When vets perform procedures on small animals, it is often safer to restrain them rather than anesthetize them.

JENNY KROLL   *Veterinary Technician*

Jenny Kroll works as a zoo veterinary technician. She trained for two years in the vet tech program at the University of Cincinnati College of Medicine before her real hands-on training began at the Cincinnati Zoo. Working side by side with the zoo veterinarians, Jenny provides care to some of the rarest animals on Earth. She works daily with Sumatran rhinos, lowland gorillas, and Komodo dragons, to name just a few. Among her many responsibilities are administering drugs prescribed by a vet, drawing blood, and assisting with surgery. In addition to working with the zoo's vets, Jenny consults with animal keepers, curators, and nutritionists to make sure that the collection is receiving the best care possible. With a huge zoo collection of thousands of animals, much of her task involves preventative medicine. By keeping regular records of weights,

diet, medications, and breeding habits, the veterinary team keeps the animal collection active and healthy.

injured wildlife generally do that part of their work as a labor of love. If you volunteer with a local vet and show enough interest and initiative, eventually you'll get to go along and assist on such special cases.

Field veterinarians work with exotic animals *in situ*, or "in nature." These women and men generally are experts in exotic animal anesthesia, which is especially important in game capture and population management. Few field vets have full-time jobs.

Those who do are typically employed by a national park system. However, many exotic-animal vets take part in field studies from time to time, while maintaining a full-time job "back home" at a zoo or related institution. Field veterinarians often assist scientists in the capture and release of study subjects and in collecting samples of blood, parasites, or other materials for future analysis. And for special cases of highly endangered species, such as the mountain gorilla of Central Africa, the field vets work in programs set up to monitor and protect the health of the animals.

Research veterinarians work with exotic animals in universities, at corporate laboratories, and other research centers, to provide long-term health care for the study animals.

At least four years of college and another four years of veterinary school are required to earn a Doctor of Veterinary Medicine (D.V.M.) degree. As in any field of modern medicine, there are a variety of specialties in veterinary medicine, each requiring additional training. Look under "veterinarians" in a big-city phone book and you'll find veterinary surgeons, orthopedists, ophthalmologists, and even cardiologists. These specialists lend their expertise to help zoo or aquarium vets with specific cases. Sometimes exotic-animal vets even call in M.D.'s for interesting cases such as diabetes or high-risk pregnancies.

Veterinary technicians perform jobs that are just as vital and diverse as those of the nurses and physicians' assistants and medical technicians who care for people. Vet techs perform a wide variety of medical procedures, particularly in zoo or aquarium settings, where there are often large and diverse collections of animals. There is no typical "day in the life of" a vet tech. Most often veterinarians and vet techs work side by side, consulting with one another on the best treatment for an animal. Among the duties of a veterinary technician are administering drugs and other treatments as prescribed by the vet; keeping

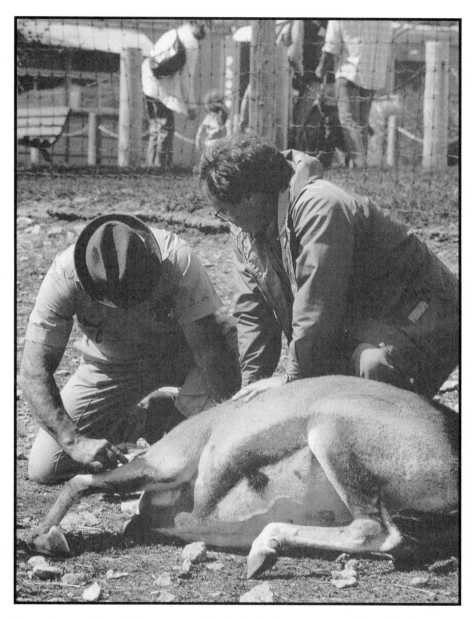

Sometimes vets and keepers conduct physical exams or perform simple procedures on large animals right in their exhibits.

records on treatments; consulting with animal keepers, trainers, or pet owners; assisting the veterinarian with surgery and other medical procedures; and performing lab work.

A minimum of two years of college are required to earn a vet tech degree, but as with many technical careers, continued education and experience are important components of performing this job successfully. Check out the requirements of the vet tech program at a college near your home. Many universities and community colleges offer two-year training programs for this field. That may sound easy enough, but the programs require math and chemistry so you'll going to need to keep studying just to get admitted! Many vet techs eventually go on to complete their four-year college degree.

	SCHOOLING	INCOME
Veterinarian	1 2 3 4 5 6 7 8 9 10	1 2 3 4 5 6 7 8 9 10
Vet tech	1 2 3 4 5 6 7 8 9 10	1 2 3 4 5 6 7 8 9 10

HOW TO USE SCHOOLING AND INCOME CHARTS

Throughout the book you will find charts like the one above. They illustrate the training required and the typical income opportunities for particular careers. The schooling column refers to average years of college and graduate school, and the income column measures income relative to other jobs in this book. For example, a schoolteacher has to have 4 years of college and would earn about a 4 in relative income, while a lawyer needs 4 years of college plus 3 of law school (for a total of 7 in the schooling column) and earns about a 7 or 8 in relative income. Remember these numbers are averages, for training and income. There are always possibilities for additional training, and income may vary significantly depending on the institution you work for and on your skills.

College guidebooks are a great place to start when looking into the educational requirements for certain careers. Two comprehensive guidebooks are *The Fiske Guide to Colleges* and *The Insider's Guide to the Colleges.*

Try Taking This Quiz . . .

Which are you more interested in?

Owning your own Lear jet.	Creating your own adventures.
Seats on the fifty-yardline at the Super Bowl.	Learning about animal behaviors
Making millions of dollars.	Making a difference.
Having a big office.	Exploring new places.

Field biologists and researchers typically live for periods of time in remote and sometimes solitary wilderness areas.

This little quiz may seem silly, but it's good to think about what is important to you before you go to college or graduate school. For example, if you work in wildlife management or biology, you won't get most of the things in the left column. But you will get many chances to do the work you care about, as well as to meet and work with people with similar interests.

two
ZOO AND
AQUARIUM CAREERS

*The purpose of modern zoos is to encourage people
to get involved and support the protection of nature.*
—Terry Maple, Director, ZooAtlanta

Keepers have the jobs most people picture when they think
of working in a zoo or an aquarium. They are the direct caregivers for the animals and the first line of defense when an animal needs health care. But the job of a zookeeper is much more
complex than just feeding and cleaning up after animals.

Keeping animals is still hands-on work. Modern farmers may
use technology to help them manage their farms, but at the end
of the day most farmers are plenty tired from long hours of physical exertion. It is the same for zookeepers who spend a good part
of each day maintaining exhibits, preparing diets, and working
with and cleaning up after their animals. It is hard, physical work
that requires a great deal of attention to detail. For example, in
addition to large mammals, many zoos today have collections of
small animals—insects, spiders, and other invertebrates—which
require as much care as any of the larger, more familiar zoo animals, often much more. But no matter the species, good keepers
are a blend of caregiver, animal handler and trainer, researcher
and expert on the creatures in their care. In order to give an

animal the proper captive environment, a zookeeper must know what its habitat and nutritional requirements are and must understand the specifics of its behavior. For example, if a monkey spends most of its waking hours in the wild foraging for food, it is healthier to feed it lots of little portions of food spread around its exhibit than to simply give it one big meal a day in a food dish.

There has been an amazing evolution in the work of the zookeeper during the last fifteen years. The field has moved from the "art" of taking care of animals to the "science" of taking care of animals. Decisions are made not because someone "feels" it's the right time to put certain animals together, but because they have data suggesting that it "is" the right time.

A great deal can be learned about the insides of an animal from the outside. Here a behavioral researcher collects a urine sample from a South American white-faced saki, in order to study its hormones and reproductive cycles.

Bugs are wildlife too! A high school student gets real-world experience working with Australian walking-sticks (right) and sunburst diving beetles (below).

33

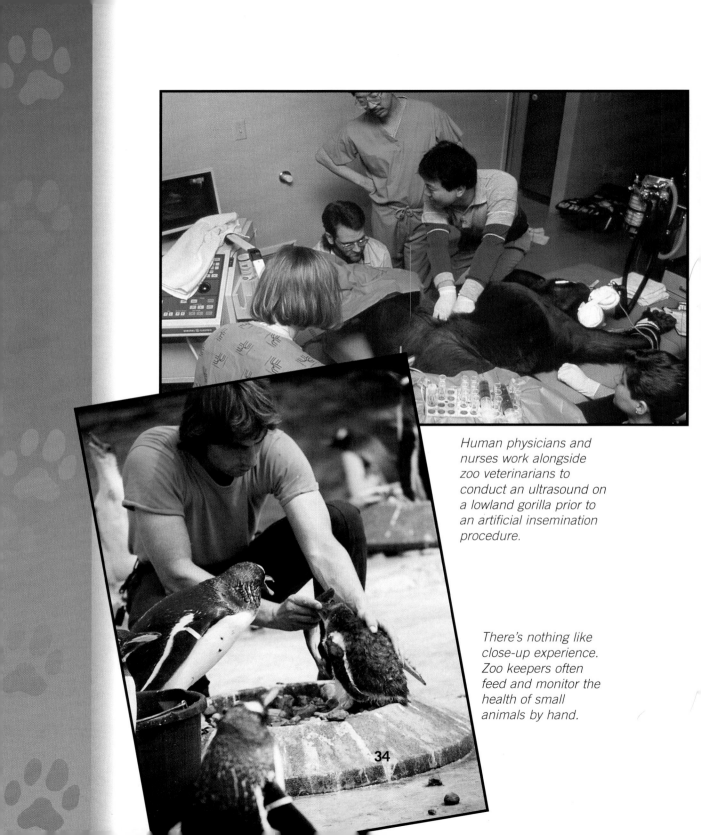

Human physicians and nurses work alongside zoo veterinarians to conduct an ultrasound on a lowland gorilla prior to an artificial insemination procedure.

There's nothing like close-up experience. Zoo keepers often feed and monitor the health of small animals by hand.

34

Because even the largest animals in the zoo are sometimes closely worked with, training is an important part of an animal's husbandry routine.

Exotic animals can become habituated to people. One of the few remaining black rhinos in central Kenya is under round-the-clock watch to protect it from poachers.

35

Whales may be predators, but they'll do almost anything for a fish. Training of marine mammals, such as this beluga whale, allows a veterinarian to conduct a physical exam without confining or anesthetizing the animal.

By providing a reward system of food treats, trainers are able to work with otherwise untractable animals. This cheetah is part of the Cat Ambassador Program which allows thousands of school students each year to get close-up views of exotic cats.

Sometimes wildlife is studied from a distance. Biologist Stan Rullman records the sounds of tropical birds in the forests of the West African country of Gabon.

Herpetologist Johnny Arnett is an expert on the Komodo Dragon, the largest lizard in the world. Here he prepares to weigh and measure the eggs of this dangerous predator.

Wildlife photographers and biologists will crawl through mud or worse to get the shot; as here, photographing a rare reptile—Amphis biana—in a South American rain forest.

Even African elephants, the largest of all land animals, are studied by remote telemetry. The elephant herds often walk great distances each day. Radio tracking allows researchers to study their behavior without bothering the animals.

Russ Mittermeier, primatologist and president of Conservation International, is leading the effort to protect biologically diverse ecosystems.

Merlin Tuttle, founder and president of Bat Conservation International, has worked to raise public awareness of the importance of protecting bats.

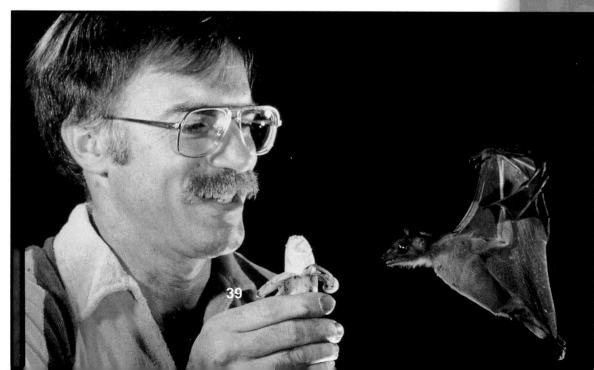

39

Bio-prospecting field researchers collect specimens of tropical plants for a study of their potential medicinal use. These leaf samples will be flown to laboratories for analysis.

Zoo educators also work in the classroom. Dave Jenike tells the story of the comeback of the American alligator to a fourth grade class.

40

ROBIN SAUNDERS *Zookeeper*

Most zookeepers are experts on their animals. They know about each species, and they even know the individual characteristics of each animal in their care. Robin Saunders is that kind of keeper. She is an expert in amphibian husbandry. Under her care, the Cincinnati Zoo has developed one of the primary frog and toad breeding programs in the world. She has successfully bred animals that were on the verge of extinction, such as the Wyoming toad, and has a huge breeding group of poison dart frogs, each one of which needs specific, individual care. But Saunders didn't set out to be an amphibian keeper. She got her training at the National Zoo in Washington, D.C., where she hoped to be a herpetologist, or reptile specialist. The reptile keepers

at the National Zoo would sometimes joke about frogs and other amphibians, referring to them as "bait" and "snot skins," a reference to their mucus-covered skins. But Saunders was asked to work with their amphibian keeper, and her future path was set. That apprenticeship led to a career of studying and caring for amphibians.

Much of Saunders' day is spent in the Froggery, an amphibian breeding facility with adjustable humidity, light, and temperature. Some frogs have such specific needs that she has to simulate rainstorms during their breeding season in order to get them together. Saunders also works with the largest amphibians on Earth, the giant salamanders of China and Japan. At over four feet in length, these predators are extremely rare and extremely aggressive. So when she feeds them their fish, Saunders makes sure that she keeps them at more than arm's length. She also participates in biological field studies of frogs in some of the hottest and most remote regions of South America.

In addition to her skill with the animals under her care, Robin Saunders is willing to share her knowledge with others. Even after a very brief conversation with her, I walk away having learned something new about amphibians.

Keepers don't just keep animals, they also keep records. Monitoring the health of animals requires attention to detail, not just "seat of the pants" intuition about a creature's condition. For most animals in zoos and aquariums, there are elaborate, detailed records chronicling their diet, weight, growth, and behavior. The keepers work directly with the veterinary and curatorial staffs to monitor changes in an animal's health or diet. Whether maintained as written charts and files or on a computer, these records are essential for the long-term care of the collection—that is, the zoo or aquarium animal population. Up-to-date record keeping insures that everyone has the information necessary to make the best decisions for the animals.

One important tool used by animal keepers is called ARKS, or Animal Records Keeping System. It is a computer-based record-keeping system that offers tremendous advantages over the old written system. Its records are uniform, so throughout a zoo or aquarium, or even in different institutions or foreign countries, the records are easy for everyone to understand. And as the records may be easily accessed via computer, keepers or health-care staff can get information on a regular basis and get it quickly. In the old system, the keeper might have had to wait until the one person who understood how to find the information was available.

Another important area of animal husbandry that is primarily the zookeeper's responsibility is **animal enrichment**, or providing a healthier, less stressful, and more active captive

A keeper weighs a king penguin chick. Weekly weight records are important indicators of a zoo animal's health.

ANDY BAKER   *Zoo Curator*

*A*ndy Baker is a modern curator's curator— experienced, educated, published, involved in the field as well as the zoo. He serves as Curator of Primates and Small Mammals at the Philadelphia Zoo. An expert on small primates, he has a Ph.D. in zoology from the University of Maryland and a degree in biological sciences from Stanford University. More important for his job as curator, he has more than ten years of experience managing animal collections and is a published expert on parental care in captive mammals. Key among the daily tasks he undertakes are the supervision of the keepers in his division at the zoo and the overall management of and planning for the institution's primate and small mammal collection. His responsibilities also include the planning of new exhibits and the evaluation of existing ones to see that they are accomplishing their educational goals. Animals are not simply placed in

zoos at random or to fill up space. The principal mission of a modern zoo is public education, and it is up to the curator to make sure that the institution has the animals necessary to effectively communicate the theme of each exhibit.

environment. By reinforcing natural behaviors and reducing boredom in captivity, the overall health of an animal is improved. Enrichment is a growing area in zoos and aquariums, partly because of many new laws protecting captive animals. As a result, some institutions have created jobs directed at animal enrichment.

JOAN EMBERY

Goodwill Ambassador for the San Diego Zoo

Joan Embery is the most famous zoo personality in the world. She works for the San Diego Zoo as an animal trainer and handler, and she escorts all types of wildlife all over the world. She is the author of three books, has thirty years of experience, and has represented her zoo on all seven continents. But she is most renowned for her hundreds of appearances on "The Tonight Show." She and her animals have been on the television program—first with Johnny Carson and then with Jay Leno—more than any other guest. Through these appearances and the hundreds of other lectures and programs she gives each year, Joan has reached many millions of people with her message about wildlife.

Embery started working in the children's zoo at the San Diego Zoo when she was a teenager. One of her first responsibilities was to train an Asian elephant, and she was so successful at learning the necessary skills that she gave elephant shows at the zoo for years. The trained elephant was also the start of her television career. Today, animals are still central to her life. On her ranch in southern California she has a variety of horses—including Clydesdales, miniature ponies, and cutters—as well as cheetahs, zebras, and even a giraffe that she takes on television! Joan Embery really does live with her work.

RICH BLOCK   *Communicator*

R ich Block is director of the Santa Barbara Zoo. In addition to planning and coordinating a wide variety of programs and exhibits for the zoo, he is a remarkable lecturer and TV host for wildlife programs. Best known for his passionate presentations on wildlife conservation, Block has organized effective programs all over the world. Working with the World Wildlife Fund, the U.S. Fish and Wildlife Service, the Dian Fossey Gorilla Fund, and the American Zoo and Aquarium Association, Block has built lasting partnerships that spread the word about what it takes to protect wildlife. Believing that solid scientific information concerning endangered species is far too important to keep hidden in hard-to-find journal articles, he developed a partnership between the U.S. Fish and Wildlife Service and the University of Michigan School of Natural Resources and Environment, to make the monthly publication "Endangered Species Update" available to the general public.

Block's training for his work includes a B.S. degree in biology from Principia College and a master's degree in natural resources and environmental communication from the University of Michigan.

Aquarists are specialized keepers of creatures that live in the water. They perform a wide variety of duties—some of which require specialized training—to care for and manage the animals in a modern aquarium. Depending on their expertise, aquarists work with many different kinds of fish, from sharks to seahorses, as

45

well as with all sorts of aquatic invertebrates, from lobsters to coral.

Training and experience in chemistry is important for aquarists, who monitor the water conditions in their collections' tanks daily. Aquarists in charge of large tanks often need to be certified scuba divers because they need to work underwater in order to keep the exhibit a clean and healthy environment. Using scuba equipment also enables aquarists to get up-close views of the habitats in which their animals live in the wild. This underwater experience is invaluable for understanding how to care for aquatic animals.

Today most animals in zoos and aquariums are born in captivity and exchanged from one institution to another for breeding and exhibition purposes. However, expeditions are still launched to collect some animals, particularly aquatic animals. Aquarists and other scientists working in aquariums need experience on ships and underwater in order to learn to capture and handle fish and aquatic animals. Three of the reasons that we now collect more aquatic than land animals are (1) there are so many different kinds of aquatic animals out there, and (2) we still have a great deal to learn about the breeding cycles, behavior, and needs in captivity of many aquatic species, and (3) we can get them, since there are no laws protecting them.

For example, there are more known species of fish (30,000) than all other vertebrate species combined (22,400). A great deal more research and experience is needed to better understand the complexities of fish and other aquatic animals.

Animal trainers work directly with hundreds of different types of animals; most often marine mammals, elephants, birds, and both large and small cats. They use a variety of techniques to maintain tractable, or handleable, animals. Sometimes wild animals are trained for use in animal demonstrations at zoos or aquariums or in educational programs at schools. But gone are

As part of an aquatic ecology research project, an aquarist collects fish specimens on a tropical expedition.

SHARON MATOLA

Director of the Belize Zoo and Tropical Education Center

THE NATIONAL ANIMAL OF BELIZE
CENTRAL AMERICAN TAPIR,
Tapirus bairdii

and why wildlife and wild areas are important to people. Today the fifty-acre zoo is so successful in that mission that it is often mentioned as a model zoo, along with the much larger Bronx Zoo, Arizona Sonora Desert Museum, San Diego Wild Animal Park, and Disney's Animal Kingdom.

The Belize Zoo started with a dream. I refer to Sharon Matola as one of the best conservationist role models on Earth because she does not take "no" for an answer. When she first proposed the establishment of the Belize Zoo she didn't just talk about it, she got going. She began with a menagerie left over from the filming of a wildlife documentary TV series. With fierce determination, hard work, and the help of many sponsors, Matola demonstrated that she and her zoo were in Belize to stay. Now the children of Belize learn about wildlife from the zoo's programs every day.

*S*haron Matola founded the Belize Zoo and Tropical Education Center in 1982. Just outside Belize City, the largest town in this Central American country, the zoo is run by, and for, Belizeans. Its mission and its message is education: to provide the people of Belize with a chance to learn about the wildlife of their beautiful country and to explain how

the days when chimpanzees rode bicycles in animal shows in zoos. Today most shows demonstrate the amazing adaptations of exotic animals. They display natural behaviors, such as the flight of birds or the running or jumping abilities of wild cats. These show animals need daily care and reinforcement from their train-

TONY VECCHIO *Zoo Director*

Zoo directors wear many hats. Some say that directors are like circus jugglers, keeping an impossible number of balls in the air. But somehow they succeed.

Tony Vecchio is a good example of a modern zoo director. He is well educated, with a bachelor's degree in wildlife management and conservation from Pennsylvania State University and a master's degree in biology from the University of South Carolina, and he started as a keeper. So he knows about animals—about their exhibition, care, and breeding. Just as important, he knows about people. As director of the Oregon Zoo in Portland, he has to manage and motivate hundreds of employees, from veterinarians and research scientists to the people who run the restaurant and gift shop.

What Vecchio brings to the job is an innate sense of balance. He has a clear vision of where the zoo is going and the ability to communicate that vision to its team, the zoo staff.

ers and are generally housed in special training facilities where the trainers can work with them.

Animal training is also an important tool for the health and maintenance of the general collection. It can be used to make typically stressful events less stressful. For instance, many animals, from river otters to elephants, may be cared for much more easily if they are trained to respond to simple auditory or visual cues, or stimuli, allowing keepers and veterinarians to give them a hands-on health checkup. These checkups give veterinarians and vet techs a chance to look closely at the skin, eyes, ears,

49

A marine-mammal keeper uses rewards as part of the training routine with a Pacific walrus.

and nose of an animal. They also allow them to perform more difficult procedures such as drawing blood, without having to restrain the animals. However, training can be used for more than just veterinary procedures. Keepers and trainers work together to develop husbandry behaviors that are helpful in the regular care of an animal, such as when giving it vitamins or moving it from one enclosure to the next one.

The simplest and best way to train a captive animal to cooperate is through "operant conditioning," that is, using cues or signals as stimuli, and sometimes using food as a reward. Being able to get an animal, say a four-thousand-pound walrus, to come on command and roll over so a keeper or vet can check its skin is important for the health of the animal. Keepers and trainers must reinforce the behavior on a regular basis so that the animals continue to respond on command. Generally, positive reinforcement in animal training is in the form of food.

Curators are managers who oversee the collections in zoos and aquariums. Most curators also manage people, so they need to have both good animal knowledge and excellent people skills to be successful. Since these zoos and aquariums are living museums, curators play an important role in their success. While the day-to-day, hands-on care of the animals is the work of keepers, it is the curators who cooperate with other zoos and aquariums to insure the long-term health and reproductive viability of their collections. A great deal of an animal curator's time is spent planning exhibits and changes in their collection. In a zoo or aquarium setting there is usually a team of curators—curator of birds, curator of primates, curator of invertebrates, curator of fishes, and the like. Often, a general curator—sometimes with an important-sounding title like associate zoo director for living collections—will oversee the entire living collection. Years of experience are required for any of these curatorial jobs. Typically curators have at least a college degree in biology or zoology and most often a master's or Ph.D. degree with research and field experience with the specific animals under their charge. Today, curators in most large zoos have Ph.D.'s. Generally, a combination of education and years of experience working in the animal department of a zoo or aquarium prepare a person to be a curator.

Along with the ability to work with animals, and "people skills," curators must also have communication skills. For example, in order to breed many of the animals in captivity today, international cooperation is needed. Through a program called the Species Survival Plan (SSP©), zoos and aquariums work hard to insure the greatest possible genetic diversity of many of the endangered animals in their collections. Genetic diversity is a measure of how closely related two animals of the same species are. In the finite captive populations in zoos, it is very important to manage the selective breeding of animals. Generally, in zoos and in the wild, the greater the genetic diversity the better.

This is how the SSP works. The SSP management group, made up of curators and other experts on a particular species, conducts genetic and demographic analyses of the species population and makes recommendations to zoos to either breed, not breed, or transfer their animals. The recommendations are sent to the institution's representatives, usually the curators. The curators may dispute the recommendations, but since they have signed a Memorandum of Understanding, agreeing to abide by

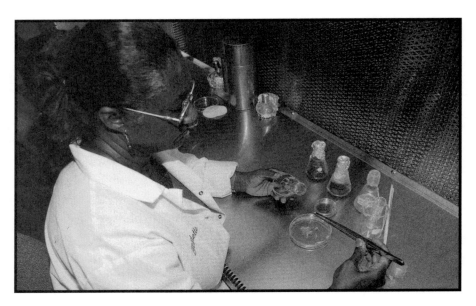

Captive breeding involves careful study to ensure genetic diversity.

the decisions of the SSP management group, generally all parties involved cooperate. Then the curator works with the zoo's registrar to complete the necessary paperwork and permits to move animals.

Once there is an agreement for a pairing, the curators work with registrars and vets to prepare breeding loan contracts, obtain certified health papers, arrange transportation, and even get international permits to bring a single animal into their collection. Moving an animal from one zoo to another in the United States may require the permission of the Department of the Interior, the Department of Agriculture, the Fish and Wildlife Service, and the Federal Aviation Administration.

A curator can be the coordinator of an SSP, as well as work on studbooks and Population Management Plans, and other programs for monitoring and managing captive breeding. Curators also work closely with the veterinary department in making long-term animal management decisions. In fact, the curator is generally the point person for all activities regarding access to the animals in his or her care. These can include marketing needs, education needs, and a variety of other concerns.

Breeding is only one of many areas of responsibility in the management of an animal collection. Sometimes not breeding is more appropriate. Contraception, or birth control, is an important technique used to insure viable populations.

Another very important responsibility is the educational message communicated by the exhibit to the zoo or aquarium visitors. It is the curator's job to insure that the appropriate animals are on display—animals that will help tell the story an exhibit was designed to tell. For example, if a display of Mexican thick-billed parrots is integral to the conservation message of an exhibit on the southwest desert, the curator needs to be sure the zoo team is cooperating with other zoos to insure that there will be ample captive-bred parrots for the future.

In addition to their work with the animals in their collection, many zoo and aquarium curators are involved in conservation projects in other parts of the world. Curators often lead the way in coordinating *ex situ* (zoo-based) and *in situ* (field-based) conservation efforts. These efforts involve more than just science; they may include everything from fundraising to organizing international seminars.

Educators seek to reach the public directly with the institution's message and mission. And while everything at a zoo or aquarium should be educational, it is the educators who direct the programs that demonstrate how nature actually works. Zoo and aquarium educators do lots of different things. Among their most important tasks are teaching classes, leading tours, and giving informal programs on animals and nature. But as with all teachers, the percentage of time spent actually teaching or leading pro-

Wildlife educators and, often, their animals, appear in a variety of settings—classrooms, zoo facilities, television talk shows and others—to introduce the public to nature. Joan Embery has played a leading role in encouraging public awareness of wildlife issues.

grams is small compared to the time required to prepare for and organize these programs. Educators and their support staff deal with the scheduling, promotion, curriculum planning, and gathering of the animals and materials required to run a successful program.

Most zoo and aquarium educators have four-year college degrees in biology or an animal-related field of study. They need a solid understanding of wildlife and natural history and a great deal of energy and enthusiasm. They are the interpreters who teach the zoo and aquarium members and visitors about the wonders of nature. It takes passion to do it well.

The position of a **zoo** or **aquarium director** represents the peak of a career; it is not a job for which one can simply train. Directors oversee all of the aspects of the organization, a job that requires years of experience, strong management skills, and in-depth knowledge of the creatures in the collection. A zoo or aquarium director is the manager of both the employees and the institution and is also the principal liaison to the community, building goodwill and raising money for the organization. Among the many skills needed to be an effective zoo or aquarium director is the ability to communicate the organization's mission and message to the community and throughout the institution itself.

Zoo and aquarium directors have diverse backgrounds. Generally directors have at least a four-year college degree in an animal-related field such as zoology, biology, or wildlife management, combined with years of experience working in similar facilities. But not all directors bring an animal background to the job. Sometimes a solid business background can help them lead an organization effectively. However, the ability to communicate the mission and purpose of the zoo or aquarium is always essential.

The American Zoo and Aquarium Association (AZA) offers a variety of professional training programs, including Professional

Management Development for Zoo and Aquarium Personnel, Studbook Management, Population Management, Conservation Education Training Program, Applied Zoo and Aquarium Biology, and Principles of Elephant Management. These graduate courses are offered for zoo employees currently working in the field as a way to promote professional development and advancement. For example, a keeper hoping to eventually become a curator might take Professional Management and Population Management as preparation for the future.

	SCHOOLING (1–10)	INCOME (1–10)
Zookeeper Aquarists	1 2 3 4 5 6 7 8 9 10 (shaded 1–4)	1 2 3 4 5 6 7 8 9 10 (shaded 1–4)
Animal Trainer	1 2 3 4 5 6 7 8 9 10 (shaded 1–4)	1 2 3 4 5 6 7 8 9 10 (shaded 1–4)
Curator	1 2 3 4 5 6 7 8 9 10 (shaded 1–6)	1 2 3 4 5 6 7 8 9 10 (shaded 1–5)
Zoo Educator	1 2 3 4 5 6 7 8 9 10 (shaded 1–4)	1 2 3 4 5 6 7 8 9 10 (shaded 1–4)
Zoo/Aq. Director	1 2 3 4 5 6 7 8 9 10 (shaded 1–6)	1 2 3 4 5 6 7 8 9 10 (shaded 1–7)

three

RESEARCH

What is now proved was once only imagined.

William Blake

Scientists are curious people. Instead of sitting around like bumps on a log, they are more likely to turn the log over to see what's growing underneath. They pursue questions that interest them and seek to understand the world around them. The scientific process involves carefully documented observation and experimentation. But scientists don't know it all. They constantly ask questions, and they often get the answers wrong. The secret to a successful career as a scientist is to keep asking the questions.

Hundreds of career choices are possible in the field of wildlife research. The work can vary, but the process remains quite similar. In today's world most of the jobs in research involving wildlife require at least one college degree and often more. Most wildlife biologists have a general undergraduate science degree, typically in biology. They then focus their interest, research, and experience in more specific areas of study while obtaining a master's degree and a doctorate. It may sound like a lot of schooling, but remember that to be a researcher you must be interested in finding the answers to specific questions. Once

TERRI ROTH — *Reproductive Physiologist*

Dr. Terri Roth is director of the Center for Research of Endangered Wildlife (CREW) at the Cincinnati Zoo. She leads a team of veterinarians and physiologists who use medical techniques such as artificial insemination, embryo transfer, and cryogenics (the effects of very low temperatures) to learn more about wildlife reproduction. Roth prepared by getting a degree in biology from the University of California at Davis and a master's degree and doctorate in reproductive physiology from Louisiana State University.

Roth has worked with a wide variety of species during her career, from snow leopards to Asian elephants. Perhaps her most challenging and exciting work to date has been with the Sumatran rhinoceros. These small forest rhinos, weighing only 1,000 to 2,000 pounds, are the most endangered animals in captivity, and Terri Roth is one of the few people able to work directly with them. Through the intense study of the female Sumatran rhino's reproductive cycle, she has been able to make significant contributions to our knowledge of rhino behavior. By studying the hormone levels in females, Roth has been able to very accurately predict when they will ovulate, or produce eggs. So, by synchronizing the introduction of the males to the females, she greatly increases the chances of successful breeding. So far, Roth's work has resulted in two pregnancies, with great hopes for successful Sumatran rhino births in the future.

you're on your way you'll find you are becoming an expert and will be able to explore those questions through your career.

The wildlife career I have been asked about the most after veterinary medicine is that of **marine biologist**. I believe this is due to the eternal human fascination with the sea, but whatever the reason, the field of ocean research is, indeed, a captivating one. Marine biologists do much more than just scuba dive and rescue whales and manatees. Any aspect of ocean life may fall within the scope of a marine biologist. Researchers do, however, need to choose a specific field of expertise on which to focus. Marine biologists may study things as varied as bacterial blooms, such as the "red tides," or the growth rates of coral reefs around the world.

University programs in marine biology are extremely competitive and require success in chemistry, physics, and math, in addition to general knowledge about the ocean realm of animals and plants. After the completion of your undergraduate and graduate training, the study of aquatic life can be extremely rewarding. Employers of marine biologists include the National Oceanic and Atmospheric Administration (NOAA); conservation organizations, such as the Nature Conservancy and the Center for Marine Conservation, that conduct coral reef studies around the world; and private corporations managing marine fisheries and other resources.

Physiologists are scientists who study the physical structures of living things. They can be involved in a variety of plant and animal research programs. Most physiologists have graduate degrees, typically a doctorate degree, which requires eight to ten years of college and graduate school. Reproductive physiologists work to gain a better understanding of the breeding cycles of animals. In a zoo setting this is particularly challenging since little is known about many of the species. This work is more important than ever since some species will not be taken out of the wild very much, if

Radio telemetry is an effective method of conducting behavioral research in a dense tropical forest. Here, Dr. Andy Baker tracks monkeys in South America.

at all, in the future. Some creatures are so critically endangered that they must be managed where they live in their native habitat. In order to insure that we can protect endangered animals such as gorillas and rhinos and still have them around a hundred years from now, it is important to maximize efforts to protect them.

This brings us to the important work of the **geneticist,** a scientist who studies the genetics, or relatedness, of animals and plants. Equipped with doctorates in genetics, geneticists work primarily in the laboratory, using microscopes and computers. These scientists study species from the inside, looking at the chromosomes and DNA of living things to determine the relatedness or genetic

JANE GOODALL

Chimpanzee Researcher

Dr. Jane Goodall is the most famous field biologist in the world. Her forty-year field study of the chimpanzee is the longest-running behavioral study of wild animals yet conducted. In 1961 she moved to a tent in the Gombe Forest in Tanzania and began to open a window into the wild world that people had only imagined before. Goodall was the first to document meat eating and tool use among chimpanzees. She was the first to demonstrate the complex relationships within nonhuman primate societies. And today her work continues, both at Gombe and around the world. The Jane Goodall Institute, which she heads, raises millions of dollars each year for wildlife conservation and education. In addition to her scientific research, Jane is dedicated to the vitally important task of educating today's young people. In 1992 she established the Roots & Shoots program to spread the word about wildlife conservation to young people all over the world. With headquarters in Dar es Salaam, Tanzania, the Roots & Shoots program is used in schools and nature clubs in many nations of the world. You can find out how to get involved by contacting the Jane Goodall Institute, Box 14890, Silver Spring, Maryland 20911-4890. Or check out the Roots & Shoots Web page: www.gsn.org/project/jgi/index.html.

makeup of individuals and the species. The work of the geneticist is increasingly essential due to the extremely small populations of many endangered species. Species with fewer than one thousand individuals remaining—such as California condors, Sumatran rhinos, mountain gorillas, and giant pandas—present difficult challenges to the conservationists who work to protect them. Geneticists can tell how closely related the remaining individuals are and provide other important information for their management.

Population biologists have a level of training similar to that of geneticists, but may earn a Ph.D. from a program in wildlife management, conducting very specific research on population biology. Instead of looking at the inside of the species, they generally study specific populations of animals or plants and, in cooperation with geneticists, work to determine the best strategies for the management of the group. Population biologists can help in the selection of which animals to breed with which to insure genetic diversity and to help preserve a population over the long term.

Captive breeding is not random anymore. Through the use of planning programs such as the SSP, studbooks, and Population Management Plans, it is more like a global, computerized dating game. A studbook is a bit like a pedigree. It contains all the known family heritage (parents, grandparents, birth dates, location) for all of the captive population of a given species. Population Management Plans are voluntary programs that enable population biologists to take into account the genetic, demographic, and social needs of each animal in order to make the best recommendations

ANNE SAVAGE   *Animal Behaviorist*

on the tiny cotton-top tamarin, a monkey from northern Colombia. Each year Savage travels to the forests of South America to work with a team of Colombian researchers who run a program called Proyecto Tití, which works to protect the remaining forests in which the cotton-tops live. To be effective, Proyecto Tití must be involved in more than just research. The scientists work with local villagers to develop alternatives to clearing the forests, such as introducing the use of bindes, a simple but efficient cookstove made of clay that requires only 33 percent of the wood normally used to cook a meal. Savage's team in Colombia also coordinates a variety of programs for local children, getting them directly involved with the forests near their towns so that they may develop a better understanding and appreciation of the world in which they live. Savage trained to be a scientist by earning a bachelor's degree and Ph.D. in psychology and animal behavior from the University of Wisconsin.

Dr. Anne Savage is a conservation biologist at Disney's Animal Kingdom. In this capacity she coordinates research projects all over the world—from studies of elephant behavior in South Africa to habitat use of native species in Florida. Her own research focuses

about the animal's future. SSPs are not voluntary, but are agreed to by zoos accredited by the American Zoo and Aquarium Association (AZA). Animals are managed and pairs are matched up by teams of experts with the aim of promoting the greatest genetic diversity within a captive population, even when that population is

EDUARDO ALVAREZ CORDERO
Harpy Eagle Researcher

Dr. Eduardo Alvarez-Cordero is a practical man. He is an eagle researcher from Venezuela who works with the people who live where harpy eagles live in order to protect these very endangered birds. Harpy eagles are the largest of the forest eagles and one of the biggest of all birds of prey. Unfortunately, their forests are being cut down for timber and paper production. So, Alvarez-Cordero, who founded the Harpy Eagle Conservation Program, has initiated a bold strategy to protect the remaining nests. Using GPS technology—the Global Positioning System—he pinpoints exactly where the eagles' nests and hunting areas are. GPS uses satellite technology to locate exact points anywhere on Earth. By sharing this information with loggers in Central and South America, Alvarez-Cordero helps protect the nest trees by convincing the loggers to leave a buffer zone of forest around each one. It is a compromise that may work for both the eagles and the loggers. Alvarez-Cordero trained for his work at the University of Florida, where he earned a doctoral degree in wildlife ecology.

spread all across the world at dozens of different zoos. The combination of creating a favorable age structure within a global population of animals, along with managing the breeding based on how closely related each animal is to other potential breeders in the population, reduces the risk of inbreeding problems and helps to insure self-sustaining captive breeding populations.

In addition to working on captive breeding in zoos, population biologists use the same principles to help manage wild populations. After determining the sustainable carrying capacity of an area, or how many of each species an area can support, they propose ways to control or maximize the number of plants or animals in that area.

Plants Are Wildlife, Too!

Much wildlife research involves plants. Plants are the principal components of ecosystems, and all animals depend either directly or indirectly upon plants for their survival. **Ecologists** and **field biologists**, particularly, conduct their research in the context of a natural ecosystem, studying the entire living (and nonliving) community around them. **Botanists** and **plant physiologists** study the inner workings of plants, gaining a better understanding of their reproduction and habitats.

Ethologists are scientists who study animal behavior, thus they are also called animal behaviorists. Behaviorists can work with any animal. In fact, far more behaviorists study invertebrates than study big, hairy mammals. Generally these scientists, like the majority of researchers, earn a Ph.D. in the process of training for their careers. In addition to their schooling, behaviorists need a great deal of experience actually observing animal behavior. Typically, much of this research is done in the field, but today behavior can also be monitored from remote locations by means of radio

An elephant researcher observes behavior patterns in Amboseli National Park in Tanzania.

and satellite telemetry, or using electronic transmitters and receivers to collect data. And behaviorists often work with captive populations as well, in zoos, aquariums, or research labs.

Many scientists work with captive animals prior to going into the field because they may be able to gain insight into an aspect of behavior that they couldn't study as well in the field. For example, when studying vocalizations in the wild—given all the background noise—many soft calls cannot be distinguished. In captivity, however, these calls can be recorded and categorized. Many scientists then

Behaviorists also study animals in zoos. Here a scientist tests the memory of a California sea lion.

GEORGE UETZ   *Spider Behaviorist*

Dr. George Uetz studies spiders. In fact, he is one of the world's most renowned spider behaviorists. In order to study spiders he does all sorts of things—from conducting long-term field research in Mexico to observing spiders while they're watching TV. Yes, TV! He was the first scientist to discover that spiders' eyes are able to register the picture on a television set. He has researched the courtship behavior of various arachnids previously unknown to science. Uetz's research is sponsored by the National Geographic Society and the National Science Foundation. He holds a bachelor's degree in biology from Albion College, a master's degree in zoology from the University of Delaware, and a Ph.D. in behavioral ecology from the University of Illinois.

confirm the function of these calls using playback studies in the wild. Think of a camera lens—scientists zoom in close on animals in captivity, and then zoom out in the wild. Scientists also use captive animals to test technology before it is taken to the field, such as the design and effectiveness of tracking devices for monitoring animal movements or vocalizations.

Nikko Tinburgen, the creator of ethology, said, "An ethologist is a curious naturalist." And behaviorists not only must be curious, they must also be patient. Sometimes it takes years to collect enough data to understand what an animal is doing when it behaves in a certain way. In zoos, information about animal behavior is applied to enable the animals to live healthier and more natural lives. Behavioral enrichment provides stimulation for

GEORGE SCHALLER   *Field Researcher*

D r. George Schaller is a legendary field biologist. He has spent as much time in wilderness areas as perhaps any westerner alive. His research into the behavior of African lions, mountain gorillas, and giant pandas has tremendously expanded the scientific body of knowledge about the world around us. As director of research for the Wildlife Conservation Society, Schaller has conducted long-term field studies around the globe. His recent work has taken him to the most remote regions of Mongolia, where he is studying endangered hoofed animals, including the traditional beast of burden, the Bactrian camel.

Schaller prepared for his life in the wilderness through his education at the University of Wisconsin and the University of Alaska. In addition to being a prolific researcher, Schaller is a wonderfully articulate writer, beautifully evoking the splendor of Earth's remaining wilderness areas. His books include The Last Panda, The Year of the Gorilla, *and* The Serengeti Lion. *In addition, Dr. Schaller's research was chronicled in Peter Matthiessen's award-winning book,* The Snow Leopard.

captive animals and promotes natural behaviors. For example, most of the exhibits in a modern zoo are planned to reflect aspects of a species' natural behaviors. Sometimes this is as obvious as reversing the light cycles for nocturnal animals or providing climbing trees for arboreal animals. But some enrichment programs are more subtle, like varying the types and location of food provided for particular animals. Since most primates spend much of their days in the wild searching for food, caregivers for many zoo gorillas, orangutans, and other primates scatter small bits of food around their exhibits, and do this more than once a day instead of giving them a single daily feeding on a plate.

Endocrinologists are scientists who study the endocrine system (including glands and hormones) of the body and its functions. This work is a medical subspecialty and requires a medical degree or a Ph.D. in endocrinology. However, their research does not always require surgery or other medical procedures. Endocrinologists are scientists, but they act like detectives, studying natural clues to answer questions about wildlife. Most of the endocrinologists who work with wild animals study reproductive endocrinology. They conduct tests called assays to determine the composition of animals' hormones in order to learn more about the reproductive capabilities of a species. Often the assays are run in laboratories, but much of the work of endocrinologists is done in zoos or natural habitats. They can run chemical tests on an animal's blood, but most often these scientists collect urine, feces, and saliva to use in their tests. That may sound a little gross, but endocrinologists' research has made it possi-

It is vital for biologists to record as much information as possible while in the field so they can later compile and publish accurate data.

69

GARY NABHAN *Ethnobiologist, Writer, Storyteller*

Dr. Gary Nabhan is director of science and conservation at the Arizona Sonora Desert Museum in Tucson. He conducts his principal research in the Sonoran Desert of Mexico and the American Southwest, exploring the relationships between people and the plants and animals upon which they depend. The author of a dozen books, Nabhan is one of the founders of the Forgotten Pollinator campaign, which is an attempt to demonstrate the interdependence of native insects and plants and the importance of this interdependence to the world around us. As a scientist, he studies the plants and animals of the desert, for which he trained by earning a doctorate in botany at the University of Arizona. As a natural history writer, he integrates human culture with nature in remarkable ways—blending anthropology, botany, ecology, and a sense of humor. Nabhan is a recipient of a MacArthur Fellowship, a Pew Scholarship on Conservation and the Environment, and the John Burroughs Medal for Natural History Contributions. His books include Cultures of Habitat, The Desert Smells Like Rain, *and* The Geography of Childhood.

ble to learn many things about the state of an animal: not just what they eat, but if they are pregnant, where they are in their breeding cycle, and how healthy they are.

Nutritionists study the makeup of animal diets in captivity. Generally a nutritionist has at least a master's degree in nutrition, or more likely a Ph.D., in addition to years of experience working with animal diets. Their work is essential since proper nutrition is important to the health of all animals. In a zoo or

EDWARD O. WILSON *Entomologist and Author*

D r. E. O. Wilson is one of this century's most renowned scientists. He is the originator of numerous fields of study in biology, including island biogeography and sociobiology. Wilson is best known for his research on ants and for his more than thirty books, including The Diversity of Life, *an important description* of the interdependence of the species with whom we share this planet. He has twice won the Pulitzer Prize for his writing. Wilson holds degrees from the University of Alabama and Harvard University. If you are interested in a great book that describes the life of a biologist in training, you should read Wilson's autobiography, Naturalist. In compelling style, he describes his youth outdoors in the American Southeast, where he first developed his own "biophilia," a term he has coined to describe the human species' innate love of nature. Wilson is a dedicated conservationist and one of the world's most articulate writers and speakers on the importance of nature to people. In his words, "The light and the way for the Earth's biological diversity is the protection of natural ecosystems."

aquarium setting the role of a nutritionist can be particularly challenging since no one is absolutely certain what some exotic animals need to eat. Generally, most zoo animals are given a diet as similar as possible to what they would eat in the wild. This is important, since, over millions of years, each species has evolved to have a digestive track built for particular foods. Happily, some animals are general feeders, such as elephants, which eat a huge variety (and a huge quantity) of plants. However, some animal species, such as Sumatran rhinos or New Guinea walkingsticks, need plants specific to their wild habitats. It is the job of the nutritionist to study the nutritional makeup of foods that might be offered, as well as to share information with other zoos, and to ask for information from zoos that have experience with certain species. The goal is to insure that each animal gets the healthiest diet possible. In addition to working directly with exotic animals, nutritionists may also find careers in research labs since today many zoo and aquarium diets are commercially prepared by companies like Purina, Iams, and Nebraska Brand Diets.

	SCHOOLING	INCOME
Marine biologist	1 2 3 4 5 6 7 8	9 10 · 1 2 3 4 5 6 7	8 9 10
Physiologist	1 2 3 4 5 6 7 8	9 10 · 1 2 3 4 5 6 7	8 9 10
Geneticist	1 2 3 4 5 6 7 8	9 10 · 1 2 3 4 5 6 7	8 9 10
Population biologist	1 2 3 4 5 6 7 8	9 10 · 1 2 3 4 5 6 7	8 9 10
Ethologist	1 2 3 4 5 6 7 8	9 10 · 1 2 3 4 5 6	7 8 9 10
Endocrinologist	1 2 3 4 5 6 7 8	9 10 · 1 2 3 4 5 6 7 8	9 10
Nutritionist	1 2 3 4 5 6	7 8 9 10 · 1 2 3 4 5	6 7 8 9 10

Feeling an adult cheetah purr is an unforgettable experience. Zoos and aquariums offer an intimate exposure to wildlife that can encourage active involvement in conservation.

Conservationists cooperate across national boundaries. George Schaller of the Wildlife Conservation Society has worked for years with biologists in China to protect the highly endangered giant panda.

Biologists (left to right) Mark Plotkin, Gary Nabhan, Beth Armstrong, and Becky Rose work with native peoples in Mexico to learn about the traditional uses of plants from the Sonoran Desert.

Radio telemetry is not only the best way to study the behavioral patterns of a rain forest cat like the jaguar, it is the only way.

74

High in a Venezuelan rain forest tree, an ornithologist checks an eagle nest.

Prey species are important too. Field biologists usually do not study a single species, but look at an ecosystem and the interrelationships among the creatures that live there.

75

The only way to study the animals and plants in the rain forest canopy is to climb up there.

The name "leopard" comes from a word meaning "to leap," as this Himalayan snow leopard demonstrates. Along with fostering a sense of wonder, animal shows impart knowledge and encourage public involvement in the protection of wildlife habitat.

WILDLIFE THEATRE
CINCINNATI ZOO

76

Volunteers and scientists work together to conduct a stream study in South America. By studying what lives in the water, biologists can determine the health of the stream. And by getting hands-on experience, volunteers can try out a career field.

Whether bird watching in your yard, or whale watching in Puget Sound, direct observation of life in the wild is one of the most rewarding activities in the world.

Biologists conducting a Rapid Assessment Program (RAP) in a tropical forest survey the diversity of the region.

Local involvement helps any project. Excitement over this snake, spotted by biologists outside a village, helped to get the people's support for a wildlife conservation project.

Learning to look: Families can better understand the variety of the Earth's plants and animals through programs and exhibits offered by zoos, aquariums, and botanical gardens.

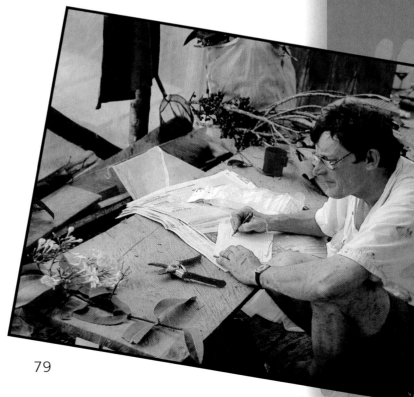

In addition to finding and shipping back specimens to a lab, field biologists make careful notes of their research in wild areas.

Field veterinary medicine must be conducted with great caution. This vet watches and waits for an elephant tranquilizer to take effect.

An early worker with wildlife, Roger Tory Peterson, pictured here with king penguins, created the first field guide in 1934.

four
EDUCATION

We must do three things to help protect biodiversity
wherever we live. . . . Educate, educate, educate . . .
argue, argue, argue . . . explain, explain, explain.

Edward O. Wilson

Environmental education careers can take many different
forms. Sometimes the work is as formal as being a full-time
classroom teacher or college professor focusing on nature and
wildlife. Other times it is as informal as being a bird-watching or
fishing guide in a national park or other natural area.

Becoming a **naturalist** is, at one time or another, the dream
of most people who love being outdoors. The thought of spending one's life "afield" is a joyous one indeed. And being a naturalist can live up to the dream. Leading nature walks, teaching
people of all ages about the flora and fauna around them, and
studying nature over a long period of time, are all wonderful pur-
suits. But to make it as an interpretive naturalist, in addition to
your love of nature, you need to possess a genuine interest in
people and be willing to spend countless hours talking, teaching,
leading, and organizing groups.

Training to become a naturalist may sometimes involve in-
depth schooling, including advanced degrees, but it always involves hundreds of days and nights spent outside—in nature!

81

WILLIAM STAPP

Naturalist and Environmental Educator

D r. William Beebe Stapp is considered the father of environmental education. He taught at the University of Michigan School of Natural Resources for more than thirty years while also serving on the United Nations Environmental Council and implementing environ-mental education programs in thirty-two countries around the world. He began his career as a naturalist with the National Audubon Society after earning a bachelor's degree in biology and has remained an ardent birder all his life. After receiving a master's degree in zoology and a doctorate in natural resources, he began his career at Michigan. In 1984 Stapp founded the Global Rivers Environmental Education Network (GREEN), a program linking young people in 135 nations all around the world and enabling them to share information about water quality in the rivers and streams near their homes. The program continues today, with kids from Israel, Jordan, India, Pakistan, and other countries sharing their interest in the water and the natural world they depend on. In 1995 Stapp was nominated for the Nobel Peace Prize.

Typically, becoming a professional naturalist or environmental educator requires the same level of education as becoming a teacher—at least four years of college.

Naturalists, environmental educators, outdoor educators—they go by many different titles, but whether they work in programs such as Outward Bound or NOLS (National Outdoor

BETTY ROSS   *Raptor Rehabilitator*

Betty Ross spends more time working directly with birds of prey than anyone I know. She is director of the Glen Helen Raptor Center in Yellow Springs, Ohio, where she is involved in rehabilitating raptors and educating the public about the importance of these birds. The Raptor Center is part of Antioch College, and many of Betty's employees are students. But the immense amount of care, feeding and medical attention that the birds require is a labor of love. Wildlife rehab is no way to make an impressive living. People entering the field must be driven by a strong desire to help wildlife and should have their eyes wide open because the responsibilities never go just from nine to five. There is really no down time at all, but there are real rewards in this work. The rewards are found in the successful release of formerly injured birds, and on the faces of kids and adults delighted by their new awareness of the natural world around them.

Betty Ross and her team at the Glen Helen Raptor Center are great examples of a successful wildlife and education program. They work only with local species, and therefore captivate people's imaginations not with a mysterious, faraway world, but with the magic found in their own backyards.

Leadership School), in a national park wearing a Smoky the Bear hat, or at the local park or nature center, their work is important. Naturalists remind us of the beauty and value of the wild world around us.

Wildlife rehabilitation is a labor of love. The pay is often low, but the rewards—whether from saving the life of an animal

The establishment of peregrine falcon populations in urban areas has raised public awareness of the plight and the dramatic recovery of this endangered species. Here, ornithologists and Division of Wildlife biologists prepare to release young falcons.

ALEX WRATISLAW   *Guide*

Alex Wratislaw is a guide in East and Central Africa. Her assignments range from the tame, like leading tours of national parks, to the wild, like launching expeditions into uncharted wilderness areas. Born in Prague and raised in England, Wratislaw was educated at Oxford University and graduated with a degree in modern languages. Her adventurous spirit and remarkable language skills have led her to live all over the world, intermittently conducting water studies for the United Nations in the Middle East or studying traditional cultures in some of the remotest regions of Africa and Asia. Today Wratislaw makes her home in East Africa but spends most of her time on expeditions into Uganda, Somalia, and Ethiopia.

Traveling in search of wildlife is a little like going fishing: you never know what you'll see. In new and unfamiliar regions, as with fishing, it is beneficial to find a guide who knows the area. Particularly in the world's remotest areas, a guide like Alex Wratislaw who knows the land and the languages is essential to a successful adventure.

that would certainly have died, or from releasing an animal back into the wild—are genuine. Though I could have discussed wildlife rehabilitation in the section on veterinary medicine, I consider "rehabers" to be educators because I think that the most important work they do is to encourage others to get involved with wildlife. Clearly, there is very high interest in and concern for animals, and even conservation. But the actual level of public involvement is still very low. Wildlife rehabilitation is one of the "on-ramps" that gives people of divergent interests a way to get involved. By working with local wildlife rehabilitators, many of whom are volunteers themselves, people become more aware of the natural areas around them and of the increasing pressures faced by the wild creatures with whom we share our world. The training for most wildlife rehabilitators is generally just hands-on experience, however, program coordinators and directors will often have college degrees and need a variety of skills to keep a program funded and viable.

Nature writers would certainly fit in the chapter called "Be Creative," but since I consider myself to be a nature writer, too—along with various other things—I count them primarily among the educators. Do not think that nature writing is confined only to books, either. In my own case, for example, I have had hundreds of pages published in books, but many thousands of pages of my writing have been in the form of television and radio scripts, signs and graphics in a zoo, or lectures presented around the world. You do not have to have had a book published to be a writer. Remember, communication is the key. More than any other medium, writing helps us to communicate our ideas. And in a world of six billion people, we need to be clear in communicating what it's going to take to save wildlife.

The best training for nature writing is to read everything you can so you know the language of writers, and to spend as much time as possible studying wildlife and the outdoors so you are fluent in the language of nature. A college degree is essential for most nature-writing jobs, so be sure to look closely at what the colleges in which you're interested have to offer. Some larger schools such as the Universities of Michigan and Wisconsin and Yale University, offer programs specifically devoted to environmental communication.

DAVID JASPER   *Nature Guide*

Dave Jasper is a professional nature guide in the American Southwest. Working out of his headquarters south of Tucson, Arizona, he reveals the intricacies of the wild desert to individuals and groups of bird-watchers, botanists, and general nature lovers. A native of rural Wisconsin, Jasper has a degree in biology from Fort Lewis College. Additional training for his career came from his work for many years with the U.S. Forest Service and the National Park System in the remote mountains of the American West.

By training himself to recognize the calls of the region's birds, and learning the Latin names of the plants in the Southwest, Jasper has insured that his tours live up to his company's name, Nature's Best. His willingness to share his knowledge and love of wild plants, animals, and places opens a window on the wild that most nature lovers would miss otherwise. One of the most exciting programs he helps to lead is Camp Chiricahua, a summer ecology and birding camp for kids, ages twelve through seventeen.

Responsible ecotourism can generate essential income for local people. Here, Russ Mittermeier and Fritz von Trong of Conservation International (rear of boat in hats) are shown potential camping sites for future ecotourists along the Sipaliwini River in Suriname.

Nature guides have remarkable jobs. They literally guide people through the magic of a natural world they might otherwise overlook. Nature guides lead field trips—for fishing, birding, and hunting, and even camera safaris on the plains of Africa. Their expertise is in the great outdoors, and that outdoors is generally their teacher as well. Guides don't require a great deal of formal schooling but it is absolutely essential that they have an in-depth, hands-on understanding of the region and the wildlife with which they're working.

Good nature guides sometimes seem like "fishing bums" or "birding bums" who never grew up or got serious jobs. But that is just part of their aura. Actually, many guides run their own small businesses, performing the scheduling, planning, and organizing tasks required for any such enterprise. In addition, guides must know about the particular animals visitors may have come to see, and good nature guides must be knowledgeable about the region's entire ecosystem—all the flora and fauna that might be encountered on the tour.

	SCHOOLING	INCOME
College professor	1 2 3 4 5 6 7 8 9 10	1 2 3 4 5 6 7 8 9 10
Naturalist	1 2 3 4 5 6 7 8 9 10	1 2 3 4 5 6 7 8 9 10
Wildlife rehabilitator	1 2 3 4 5 6 7 8 9 10	1 2 3 4 5 6 7 8 9 10
Nature writer	1 2 3 4 5 6 7 8 9 10	1 2 3 4 5 6 7 8 9 10
Nature guide	1 2 3 4 5 6 7 8 9 10	1 2 3 4 5 6 7 8 9 10

five

CONSERVATION

Never doubt that a small group of dedicated individuals can
change the world. Indeed, it's the only thing that ever has.

Margaret Mead

Conservation means the wise use of resources, and the field
of conservation is an important blend of biology and environmental policy. While people are part of the problem plaguing
wildlife today, they are also the essential ingredient in the
solution.

The field of conservation is relatively new. Before the last
century, nobody seemed to notice that we were using up Earth's
finite resources faster than they could replenish themselves.

By far the single most important thing to learn about conservation is that it always comes down to individuals. No matter
where I have traveled, from the rain forests of South America to
Yellowstone National Park in Wyoming, or the Okavango Delta
in Botswana, I have always found that it is the determination of
one or maybe two people who make a conservation project
work.

Clearly the message is this: In a world of six billion people,
individuals are not less important than they were before, but
more vital than ever. Indifference is the enemy of wildlife and

RICHARD LEAKEY

Conservationist and Paleoanthropologist

Richard Leakey's work has had a huge impact over the last thirty years both in his native country of Kenya and around the world. It has led him on the varied paths of field researcher living out of a tent in East Africa, and of government official implementing laws and regulations and influencing world opinion. As a research scientist, Leakey is one of the leading paleoanthropologists in the world, credited with finding fossils of human ancestors 2.6 million years old. Paleoanthropology is the study of humanlike creatures that predated our species, Homo sapiens. And as director of the Kenya Wildlife Service from 1989-1994, he drew worldwide support for the elephant ivory ban he implemented, and he raised over $150 million for Kenyan wildlife conservation. Leakey has been active in Kenyan politics for the last decade, and in 1998 he stepped down from parliament to take over again as director of the Kenya Wildlife Service. He is the author of more than 100 scientific journal articles on human evolution and wildlife, and his best-selling books include The Origin of Humankind, Origins Reconsidered, and The Sixth Extinction.

wild places. Left on its own, the machinery of modern commerce would strip-mine, pave over, and clear-cut everything in its path. The fierceness of individuals who stand up and say, "Enough is enough!" is what saves wild areas. It is the only thing that ever has.

Field biologists are the conservationists most of us dream of being. The Hollywood version of a field biologist drives a muddy,

FRITZ VON TRONG *Conservationist*

Fritz Von Trong is a legend. This Surinamese native is a botanical genius who knows more about the plants of his country than anyone else. Largely self-taught, von Trong has spent his life in the forest, studying the ecosystem of northern South America. He speaks five languages and is sought after for his knowledge by scientists from around the world.

Von Trong is a field biologist with Conservation International and leads research projects on the medicinal use of tropical plants. The new field of bioprospecting, or searching for renewable uses of forest plants, depends directly upon experts like Fritz von Trong, who possess a firsthand understanding of the forests and their plant species. He serves as a consultant to many organizations, herbariums, and botanical gardens around the world.

beat-up Land Rover, wears a big wristwatch suitable for deep-sea diving or circumpolar navigation, and carries a bandanna for mopping up dusty sweat.

In reality, most field biologists and conservationists have to be as skilled at manipulating a computer database or filling out a grant application as they are at anesthetizing a charging rhino or tracking the last of the California condors using radio telemetry. They need to be able to fix a truck, dig a latrine, and stay healthy in malaria-infested field sites. They are generally extremely well educated with tons of experience. And they are always broke. The adventure is high, but the pay is poor. As Wendell Berry, the poet of Kentucky, says, "The work of planet saving is humble."

A field biologists' camp in a tropical forest offers only minor protection from the elements. Among the challenges are humidity and insects, either of which can ruin computers and other electronic equipment, as well as a scientist's collected specimens.

CATHRYN HILKER   *Cheetah Conservationist*

Cathryn Hilker has Africa in her blood and has traveled there dozens of times over the last forty-five years. She is the founder and director of the Cat Ambassador Program at the Cincinnati Zoo, and a passionate and world-renowned advocate for wild cats. But forty years of teaching about conservation have taught her that talk is not enough. Her partnership with Laurie Marker, director of the Cheetah Conservation Fund, to purchase the 28,000-acre Cheetah Conservation Center in Namibia insures that, in at least one place, cheetahs will survive. Hilker recognizes that no one person alone can make conservation work. Establishing partnerships is the right method and the right message. Taking action, as Hilker puts it, is a leap of faith. When asked what led her to work to protect cheetah habitats far away in Africa, Hilker said, "Problem

solving becomes a very real thing when you move from the heart of what you love to the reality of what you must do."

Thus many field biologists are either young or work in the field part-time and in some other occupation the rest of the time to pay the bills.

The field of conservation remains blessedly unstructured, so there are no "official" job descriptions to compare. A **conservation biologist** may be someone with a Ph.D. in a sub-field of biology who is conducting research while networking with other scientists around the world. Conservation biologists

LAURIE MARKER *Cheetah Conservationist*

Laurie Marker is founder and director of the Cheetah Conservation Fund, a program with headquarters in the southwest African nation of Namibia where she has lived for the past decade. She grew up in California, received a degree in biology from the University of Southern California, and started her career in a zoo in the United States. Marker worked with a variety of animals, but her life was changed by her relationship with one cheetah. While training and giving educational programs with a cheetah named Kiam, Marker realized that she wanted to do more for the big cats, so she moved to Namibia, one of the last strongholds for cheetahs in the wild.

But in Namibia most of the cheetahs live on cattle and sheep ranches, not in protected areas like national parks. So in addition to coordinating research programs on cheetah behavior and genetics, Marker serves as honorary cheetah ambassador, demonstrating to local farmers and ranchers that people can live with cheetahs. In fact, the official motto of the Cheetah Conservation Fund is "We can live together." A principal reason for Marker's success is that she became a rancher in Namibia. As a rancher and landowner, Marker is, herself, a local, not just an expert from out of town trying to tell the locals Namibians what to do.

MARK PLOTKIN   *Ethnobotanist*

Dr. Mark Plotkin is president of the Ethno-biology Conservation Team, an organization that works with native healers and medicine men and women throughout the world. Plotkin is one of the world's premier eth-nobotanists—scientists who study the traditional use of plants by native people. Best known for his book Tales of a Shaman's Apprentice, *Plotkin works principally with remote tribes in the rain forests of South America. In preparation for his career, Plotkin received college and graduate degrees in biology and botany from Harvard, Yale, and Tufts Universities, but it was the wonders of his own backyard in New Orleans, Louisiana, that led him into the wilds of South America. He discovered his interest in conservation as a young boy, and he learned that it begins at home. As he said, "The lesson that people, especially kids, need to learn about conservation is NEVER, NEVER, NEVER give up. There are going to be disappointments. There are going to be reverses. There are going to be tragedies. But the environment is about all of us. It is about our medicine. It is about our agriculture, our industry, our religion, our spirituality. And individuals make a difference." You can learn more about Dr. Plotkin's work on the Web at: www.ethnobotany.org*

may work in a university setting or for a conservation organization or zoo, but they typically spend part of the year out in the field doing research and part of the year in a "regular" job related to wildlife and conservation. The ongoing field research of a conservation biologist is generally funded through grants, so the ability to develop and sustain funding sources is very important for success in this field. Even with grant support, conservation biologists often work with larger organizations, such as conservation groups, that also help to support their field studies.

The job of a **preserve manager**, or park manager, can be extremely rewarding and challenging work. Many of the rarest

Dr. Rodney Jackson conducts field research on the elusive snow leopards in Nepal. He, like other conservation biologists, has to practice the two "p's" of field research—patience and perseverance.

RUSSELL MITTERMEIER
Primatologist and Biopolitician

Russ Mittermeier is a powerhouse conservationist. He is president of Conservation International but a primatologist by training, and the only head of a major conservation organization who still conducts his own field research projects. Mittermeier prepared for his career by earning degrees from Dartmouth College and Harvard University, but he credits his interest in nature and natural history to his childhood visits to the American Museum of Natural History and the Bronx Zoo. He is a gifted linguist, speaking eight of the major languages and dozens of the dialects of the tropics.

Since 1990 he has discovered five new species of primates in Brazil alone. Blending scientific field research in tropical forests with biopolitics in capitals around the world, he is one of the most effective conservationists on Earth. He feels that continued research into Earth's biodiversity is essential for all of us—people and the other animals. As he puts it, "To talk about sustainable development in the face of the ignorance we have about the rest of life on Earth is rather like trying to construct a Boeing 747 with nothing but a hammer, a few nails, and a couple of sheets of scrap metal."

species remaining on Earth today live in protected nature preserves and national parks around the world. Coordinating the long-term management of these areas is a delicate balancing act—one that takes into consideration the needs of wildlife and the local people at the same time. Generally the manager of a park or preserve is someone with at least a college degree in one of the biological fields and many years of experience working with wildlife in protected parks.

Managers of conservation organizations tend to spend more time raising money than chasing after wild animals. As for the presidents of large conservation groups, such as the World Wildlife Fund, the Nature Conservancy, and the National Audubon Society—some are lawyers, some are professional managers, and a few are biologists by training. It is difficult work, comparable to running other large organizations, and the directors or presidents of these groups may be compared to presidents of small colleges. But it is important enough work that these women and men are willing to take on the challenge.

Conservation organizations also have many jobs for **program directors**. They are the managers who coordinate the work of the field staff and the support team back at the group's headquarters. A conservation program director will almost always have a college degree, and often a master's degree, in zoology or wildlife biology. Often, these positions are filled by people who have spent time out in the field, either as researchers, Peace Corps or other volunteers, or graduate students. Actual experience in the field, particularly in developing countries, helps give the program directors back home a better idea of the challenges field researchers face.

Conservation organizations offer important career opportunities for people interested in wildlife. In addition to working full time in one of the organization's offices, it is also possible to get

JACKIE BELWOOD   *Chiroptologist*

Dr. Belwood recognizes the vital relationship between insects and bats. In fact, her principal research interests involve the feeding ecology of insect-eating bats. The history of these two groups of animals are intricately tied, since most of the more than 1,000 species of bats in the world are insectivorous.

The former Science Director of Bat Conservation International, Dr. Belwood has studied bats in North America, South America, and Central America, the Caribbean, Hawaii, and the South Pacific. Among her achievements are the discovery of the first breeding colony of endangered Indiana bats in Ohio in 1996, and the building of a gigantic bat house on the University of Florida campus. It houses more than 60,000 wild Mexican free-tailed bats. She is the author of the book, Ohio's Backyard: Bats.

One of the most significant things about Jackie Belwood is her ability and willingness to communicate her knowledge and interest in bats, insects, and other wildlife. Among the most enthusiastic scientists I know, she takes the message of bat conservation and education to thousands of people every year. And she is also passionate about encouraging women to pursue careers in biology—for which she is an outstanding role model.

C hiroptologist, or bat biologist, Jackie Belwood works for the Ohio Biological Survey, studying biodiversity throughout that midwestern state. She is an expert on both insects and bats. She earned a bachelor's degree in biology from Carleton University in Ottawa, Canada, and a Ph.D. in entomology at the University of Florida.

funding for field research or conservation projects through these organizations. The best resource for learning about a wide variety of these groups is *The Conservation Directory,* a book published annually by the National Wildlife Federation in Washington, D.C.

	SCHOOLING	INCOME
Field biologist	1 2 3 4 5 6 7 8 9 10	1 2 3 4 5 6 7 8 9 10
Conservation biologist	1 2 3 4 5 6 7 8 9 10	1 2 3 4 5 6 7 8 9 10
Preserve manager	1 2 3 4 5 6 7 8 9 10	1 2 3 4 5 6 7 8 9 10
Program director	1 2 3 4 5 6 7 8 9 10	1 2 3 4 5 6 7 8 9 10
Conservation organization president	1 2 3 4 5 6 7 8 9 10	1 2 3 4 5 6 7 8 9 10

six

BE CREATIVE

If we do not have our hands on something,
what then are we doing in life?

Jonquil LeMaster

Not everybody who works with wildlife has to be a biologist. Communication is vital to wildlife conservation, and there is a greater demand than ever before for creative people who can interpret the workings of nature. As with creative people everywhere, the sky's the limit. It is entirely possible for a person to build a career as a full-time wildlife photographer, painter, sculptor, or other type of artist. In most cases, wildlife artists will need to be flexible and inventive in order to market their talents and to do more than one thing in order to insure steady income. This "don't give up your day job" career track is not essential, but it can help during slow periods when photographs or paintings don't sell.

Of course, there are many full-time jobs in which a person can use his or her creative skills in relation to wildlife. Zoos, aquariums, museums, and companies that develop exhibits for a variety of institutions all need exhibit technicians and artists to create and maintain their exhibits and interpretive displays. The past few decades have brought important technical advance-

JONQUIL LEMASTER   *Exhibit Project Manager and Artist*

To plan and build modern interpretive museum, aquarium, or zoo exhibits takes a tremendous amount of work by many people. A project manager coordinates the overall effort, keeping everyone on target and making sure that the exhibit is done right and its goals are reached. Jonquil LeMaster is an exhibit ex-pert who wears many hats. She has helped to build some remarkable exhibits, such as Jungle World at the Bronx Zoo in New York City. She is a famous fabricator of naturalistic trees and rockwork. But her principal job is to serve as a project manager. For this task she needs more than just skill as an artist. She must communicate the message of the exhibit so the team working on it understands it, and select the media to be used for it. In the planning and implementation process, her job is to coordinate the efforts of architects, engineers, sculptors, painters, writers, zoo directors, keepers, and even plumbers and electricians. It is a lot of work, but it is essential to the successful completion of the large-scale animal exhibits in today's major zoos, aquariums, and museums.

LeMaster earned a degree in art at Lewis and Clark College in Portland, Oregon.

ments that allow the building of naturalistic exhibits with realistic-looking trees, rocks, and painted murals. To get into this field, you need an understanding of natural history and the ability to simulate or represent nature and wildlife through your art.

Skills in design, sculpture, and painting are essential for the successful creation of a wildlife display or exhibit, especially if

MARCUS JACKSON   *Exhibit Sculptor*

Zoos and aquariums are thriving today, with new, naturalistic exhibits springing up in institutions all around the world. As the bars and tiled walls of the old cages are replaced by artificial rocks, streams, and trees, there is a great need for artists and sculptors who can create these displays.

Marcus Jackson is that type of sculptor. He heads the exhibit team at the Cincinnati Zoo and Botanical Garden, and his art supplies consist of concrete, steel, fiberglass, and plastic. But his job entails more than simply building the exhibits. First he makes drawings and plans. Then he builds scale models which represent what the final project will look like in three dimensions. Finally he and his team create a natural-looking home for the animals.

the exhibit will be the home of living animals. Exhibits are often modeled after photographs, but it is vital for artists to get real hands-on experience with wild places.

The training to be an exhibit artist generally involves at least a college degree in art but is best when augmented with a solid understanding of biology and natural history. You may also gain experience by volunteering or taking on an internship in college. These opportunities give a beginning artist the chance to learn about the challenges of the work.

ROGER TORY PETERSON *Author and Bird Painter*

Roger Tory Peterson, who died in 1996 at the age of eighty-seven, was a beloved wildlife artist and conservationist. His first Field Guide to the Birds, *published in 1934, revolutionized bird-watching and the study of nature and sent four generations of wildlife enthusiasts outdoors. The impact of the forty million books sold in his Peterson Field Guide series has made him the world's most important contributor to public awareness and involvement with nature. With his tiny paintbrush and his love for birds and wildlife, Roger Tory Peterson changed the way we see the world.*

Peterson's initial idea of including illustrations of key field markings in his books created a new system for identifying birds in flight. Similar species were grouped together on one page. Arrows were used to point out important field marks, such as tail spots or eye-rings, so bird watchers could identify living birds. Earlier guidebooks helped only to identify dead birds. Peterson's early work in the 1930s, establishing important bird counts at Cape May Point, New Jersey, and conducting the first African crowned eagle research in Kenya—led the way to modern ornithological field study.

ALEXIS ROCKMAN   *Painter*

Alexis Rockman is outrageous. Painting wildlife like no one since the fifteenth-century artist Hieronymus Bosch—who created fantastic, dreamlike paintings—Rockman's works are often gigantic in size and always provocative. The paintings include beautifully detailed, mysterious creatures. You can often see examples of his work in Natural History *magazine and in art gallery and museum exhibitions. They present to the world his message of the dynamic tension between nature and modern society.*

A student of both art and natural history, Rockman lives in New York City, where he grew up wandering through the halls of the vast American Museum of Natural History, an activity that clearly influenced his work. He has traveled extensively and worked afield. His art challenges many traditional views of nature. His books, Guyana, Alexis Rockman, *and* Concrete Jungle, *are good representations of his travels and paintings.*

RON AUSTING *Wildlife Photographer*

For the past five decades Ron Austing has been photographing birds around the world. He is the author of three books, including the classic World of the Red-tailed Hawk, which has been a reference for two generations of falconers and birders. Most famous for his photographs of birds in flight and capturing prey, Austing uses still photos and video to show us the world of nature.

It has taken years of experimenting out in the field for Austing to learn how to get close enough to wild animals to take his amazing pictures. He began his study of nature as a young boy in the woods near his home in southwest Ohio. By becoming very familiar with the workings of nature and the behavior of the animals around him, Austing was then able to document their behavior on film, publishing his first professional photographs while still in high school. Since then his pictures have appeared in hundreds of magazines and books, including Audubon, International Wildlife, Natural History, and the Audubon Field Guide to the Birds.

LOUISE ZEMAITIS · *Artist and Naturalist*

Louise Zemaitis is an inspiring person. She is an artist who specializes in wildlife paintings and drawings, particularly of birds. She is also is a naturalist and birding guide and works out of Cape May Point, a little town at the southernmost tip of New Jersey. Zemaitis was an artist before becoming a naturalist, getting her professional training and a degree from the Tyler School of Art at Temple University. Later, her art led her to spend years studying nature firsthand in the field in order to gain the skills necessary to become a professional naturalist and to lead nature trips around the world.

Zemaitis is inspiring because she followed her dream, moving to Cape May Point, far from the big cities where an artist normally finds employment. There surely would have been easier ways to earn a living than to pursue her art and study of nature on a daily basis, since both demand a great deal of time and commitment. Such a life makes for early mornings out in the field and late nights at the drawing table, but it also gives Zemaitis great satisfaction and makes her an in-depth naturalist and a person to be admired.

MARTIN AND CHRIS KRATT
Wildlife Television Producers

Martin and Chris Kratt are hosts of a popular TV series called "Kratt's Kreatures," which is broadcast around the world. With their incredible energy and sense of adventure, these two brothers bring wildlife programs to a new generation of television viewers. While they seem to be just a couple of wild and crazy guys out on safari, they actually are well-trained biologists who bring a remarkable blend of style and substance to their programs.

Both Martin and Chris have degrees in biology from Duke University. Upon graduation they said that they "didn't want regular jobs," so they took their mother's video camera and began making offbeat wildlife shows. They went to Madagascar and romped with the lemurs, they surfed in Costa Rica and studied sea turtles. At first they used the videotapes of their adventures to give programs in schools. Eventually the shows were broadcast on television and even won first place at the International Wildlife Film Festival two years in a row! Finally the brothers were able to start their successful series. Martin and Chris have also written a number of wildlife books for young readers. The books have the same "creature on" approach as their shows, so you might want to check them out at the library.

PETE DUNNE   *Poet and Birder*

Pete Dunne is one of the most renowned natural history writers in America. As director of the Cape May Bird Observatory, he is a tireless organizer, advocate, and communicator about the magic of wild areas.

Peter Dunne's books include Tales of a Low Rent Birder, The Wind Masters, *and* Feather Quest. *His career started when his attention and his resolve were captured by a cloud of hawks he saw flying overhead on a September day in Pennsylvania. Since that day, when the fall hawk migration directed his life to focus on the beauty and needs of birds all around the world, he has spent years observing, noting, and communicating the wonders of birds and their specific requirements for survival in a healthy, natural system.*

Dunne spends much of his time on the eastern coast of the United States in Cape May, New Jersey, writing and talking about birds and their needs.

His goal is to insure a future that will include room for birds and for the natural systems that support them. As he says, "We are all part of a community on this planet. I would like a planet that has a lot more richness than what we are heading for right now. The idea of a stark planet doesn't appeal to me at all. I don't want to be the only show in town. I don't want to go outdoors and see nothing but other people. I want to see a lot of diversity. That's why I'm out there, to keep a lot of the elements of the mosaic."

Since modern wildlife exhibits and habitats are much more complex than they were in the past, most zoos, aquariums, and museums develop exhibit teams that work to make sure the animals' needs are met and that the message the public is receiving is the one they want to send. Typically a zoo or aquarium exhibit team will consist of **zoo architects**, engineers, artists, keepers, and curators. Zoo architects, like all architects, will have completed at least four years of college and three of architecture school, while engineers will have at least an undergraduate degree in engineering.

Exhibit teams often work best when someone from the institution's interpretive or educational program is involved at the outset so that when the exhibit is finished, its message will resonate with the visitors. The same team approach is used for the development of most museum exhibits—minus the keeper, since there generally are no live animals to consider. In most bigger zoo and aquarium settings, the graphics and exhibits are coordinated by an **art director**. This person, like the conductor of an orchestra, is responsible for insuring that the pieces all fit together.

Wildlife painters and **photographers** can have wonderfully satisfying careers. The joy of creating plus the opportunity to spend time in wild places make this work enviable indeed. Some artists, such as Robert Bateman of Canada and Alexis Rockman of New York, are so well known and successful that they can afford to paint full time. Many wildlife painters paint part time and work at another job to help pay their bills. Similarly, some wildlife photographers like Ron Austing of Indiana or Art Wolfe of Seattle photograph wildlife as their sole career. Others, like Chicago-based photographer Susie Reich, shoot everything from fashion models to magazine ads in addition to their work with animals.

Museum and zoo exhibit teams work to create exhibits that will fascinate and educate visitors.

FRED SHAW   *Native American Storyteller*

*T*here are storytellers and then there are storytellers. Fred Shaw is the official storyteller for the Shawnee Nation Remnant Band, the Native American tribe to which he belongs. His stories go back thousands of years, through the history and the memories of his people. Through his work he shares the ancient wisdom of the native people with listeners of many different backgrounds. Most of the stories he tells are of the lives of animals and the lessons they have taught his people over the centuries. They demonstrate the belief that the natural world enriches and completes our lives.

Among Shaw's central themes is this idea: "The problems people face today have the solutions right beside them. We've just forgotten how to look and listen." The power of this teller of ancient stories is precisely that he helps guide those with open ears and hearts to find solutions.

Like many other storytellers, Shaw came to this traditional role through apprenticeship, studying with elders from his tribe, and listening and practicing over the course of many years.

Painters and photographers do not have to have college or graduate degrees in their fields, but many do. Their work can stand on its own if they are talented enough, but as always, experience and perseverance are what pay off in the end.

	SCHOOLING	INCOME
Exhibition technican	[1 2] 3 4 5 6 7 8 9 10	[1 2] 3 4 5 6 7 8 9 10
Exhibit artist	[1 2 3 4] 5 6 7 8 9 10	[1 2 3 4] 5 6 7 8 9 10
Architect	[1 2 3 4 5 6 7] 8 9 10	[1 2 3 4 5 6 7 8] 9 10
Art director	[1 2 3 4 5 6] 7 8 9 10	[1 2 3 4 5 6] 7 8 9 10
Wildlife painter	[1 2 3 4] 5 6 7 8 9 10	[1 2 3 4] 5 6 7 8 9 10
Wildlife photographer	[1 2 3 4] 5 6 7 8 9 10	[1 2 3 4 5] 6 7 8 9 10

seven

HOW TO GET THERE FROM HERE

When the student is ready, the teacher will appear.

Lao-tzu

Experience Is the Best Teacher

Mark Twain is credited with many great quotes. One of my favorites is "Never let your schooling get in the way of your education!" And often experience is the best education. You can volunteer at a vet clinic or nature center, for example. If you're good they'll put you to work and you may never look back! One day you'll be in college and coming back on vacations to work in your "spare" time.

Volunteers can perform all sorts of tasks. In an educational setting such as a zoo or nature center, volunteers help lead groups or teach younger kids. Generally these activities require some training, so be sure to check all your available opportunities within an organization when you sign up to volunteer. In a medical or research setting, young volunteers generally need a mentor, or at least a contact, who can help them get involved. Initially, you may simply observe the procedures performed by the experts, but if you remain interested and helpful, before long you may get to assist.

Don't Just Be Good, Be Good for Something

No matter what your age, it is very important to get involved. Don't stand around with your hands in your pockets acting cool. That is the last way to get a chance to actually help wildlife. It's OK to be eager. It's OK to show enthusiasm. If you are working with a veterinarian or a zookeeper, stay busy. Nothing impresses a mentor more than the willingness to work. And ask questions. The person you are working with has lots of experience. Ask him or her to share some of it with you so you can learn as you work.

Find a Mentor

Years ago I saw the popular movie *Bull Durham*, in which Kevin Costner plays Crash Davis, an experienced catcher on a minor-league baseball team. His main task is to help an up-and-coming pitcher get ready for the major leagues. My favorite scene is the one in which the young pitcher tells Crash how much he wants to make it big in baseball so he can buy a really fancy stereo for his car. To which Crash responds, "You don't need a stereo, YOU NEED A CURVEBALL!"

And so it is with getting started working with wildlife. It is easy to daydream about living and working on the distant

KATHLEEN STEWART *Writer, Birder, Activist*

Not everyone who works with wildlife does so to earn a living. People who devote themselves to animals and wild places are just as important to local wildlife efforts. As volunteers, committee members, board members, or as advocates for wild creatures and their habitats, these informed enthusiasts help wildlife in many ways.

Kathleen Stewart is that kind of person. She is a hawk watcher who travels everywhere she can in search of birds of prey. Every fall, for more than fifteen years, she has travelled to Cape May Point, New Jersey, for the annual hawk migration. Her first pilgrimage was spurred by Diane Kappel Smith's book, Wintering, where she read of the 100,000 hawks counted at that site each year. Since then, she

has become a life member of the Cape May Bird Observatory, working to support that organization's bird research and education programs.

Stewart's love for hawks and wild places later lead her to study the birds of southeast Arizona. Home to Harris hawks, prairie falcons, golden eagles, and a dozen other raptors, this region is one of the most biologically diverse in North America. Stirred by the beauty of the canyonlands, she became increasingly aware of the tie between wild areas and wildlife. Stewart wanted to do more than watch—she needed to help protect wildlife habitat.

As a writer, she used the written word to stop development on a 300-acre farm where she once had lived. Her essay, "To Give It A Voice," persuaded the landowners to work with the county park district to set aside the farm and keep out the bulldozers. The result is a small farm that is part of a regional greenspace. Those 300 acres remain the home of red-tailed hawks, great horned owls, red foxes, red-headed woodpeckers, and bobolinks. Without her efforts, the habitat would be gone, and so would those wild creatures.

By finding something you care about and then making it an important part of your life, you can make a real difference in the world.

A field researcher surveys his catch as part of a tropical stream ecology study.

African plains or rafting down the Amazon. But what you really need is a mentor. Someone to teach you the ropes. The trouble is that in many careers, the time-honored apprentice system no longer exists, even though it is needed more than ever. But with effort, you can find an expert who will take you under her or his wing. It is your job to learn as much as you can from that person, whether he or she is a science teacher or a researcher or a naturalist at a museum or zoo. If you demonstrate enough interest, experts will be glad to help you.

Life Is On-the-Job Training

Hundreds of programs exist to train you to study animals and plants. Some offer general biology, which is an important starting point for any wildlife field you might want to work in. Others offer specific training, such as zoology or pre-veterinary majors. But no matter what your academic focus, remember that it is important to do more than just course work. Look for opportunities to get involved with wildlife or environmental clubs or hiking, camping, or mountaineering groups. Some professors lead field studies. Be sure to take advantage of every opportunity you can find.

Some schools offering specific training include:

High School

The Zoo Academy
Cincinnati Zoo and Botanical Garden
3400 Vine Street
Cincinnati, Ohio 45220
(1-800) 944-4776, ext. 8767

Founded in 1976, the Zoo Academy is the world's oldest zoo-based high school and the only one of its kind anywhere. This

Hands-on experience is a good way to find out if working with wildlife is for you. Getting involved in field research as a volunteer or a student is also a great way to find a mentor.

four-year program offers ninth and tenth grade classes as part of the Cincinnati Academy of Math and Science (CAMAS) program. The eleventh and twelfth grades are spent at the Cincinnati Zoo and Botanical Garden. In addition to a strong emphasis on classroom work in the life sciences, the juniors and seniors spend at least two hours every day out on zoo grounds working with keepers and animals. The Zoo Academy has a college preparatory program that fulfills all the requirements for college entrance.

Animal Training

Moorpark College
7075 Campus Road
Moorpark, California 93021
(802) 378-1400

Moorpark is a world-renowned two-year college program for people who want to become animal trainers. In addition to an academic curriculum that includes biology, math, and English, students work directly with animals every day. This is no program for the lazy or distracted. Moorpark students work with their animals seven days a week, caring for them, training them, and learning through experiential education.

Animal Husbandry

Santa Fe Community College
Teaching Zoo
3000 NW 83rd Street
Gainesville, Florida 32606
(352) 395-5000

This two-year program offers a unique, hands-on approach to working with animals. The school itself is a zoo, fully accredited by the American Zoo and Aquarium Association (AZA). Students at the Santa Fe Teaching Zoo learn by doing, as they take care of the animals in the school's collection and work directly with veterinarians and curators. Graduates receive a degree in zoo animal technology.

Graduate and Undergraduate Programs

There are hundreds of college and university programs available. Here are a few that you can check out. All are very strong in biology and zoology.

University of California-Davis
Processing Service
Box 23460
Oakland, California 94623-0460
www.ucdavis.edu

Whether working to protect gray wolves in Yellowstone or cheetahs in Namibia, it is essential to build local support for conservation, as Laurie Marker of the Cheetah Conservation Fund has accomplished with local ranchers.

Cornell University Ornithology Lab
159 Sapsucker Woods Road
Ithaca, New York 14850
www.ornith.cornell.edu

University of Florida
Office of the Dean
Box 118100
330 Little Hall
Gainesville, Florida 32611-8100
www.ufl.edu
(325) 392-9230

University of Maryland
Office of Admissions
Mitchell Building
College Park, Maryland 20742-5235
www.umd.edu
(301) 314-8385

Miami University
Institute for Environmental Sciences
Campus Avenue Building
Oxford, Ohio 45056
www.muohio.edu
(513) 529-5811

University of Michigan
School of Natural Resources and Environment
430 E. University
Ann Arbor, Michigan 48109-1115
www.snre.umich.edu
(734) 764-6453

University of Washington
Office of Admissions Services
Box 355840
Seattle, Washington 98195-5840
www.washington.edu
(206) 543-9686

University of Wisconsin
Office of Admissions
750 University Avenue
Madison, Wisconsin 53706
http://wiscinfo.wisc.edu
(608) 262-3961

Yale University
School of Forestry and Environment
Registrar
205 Prospect Street
New Haven, Connecticut 06511
www.yale.edu/forestry
(203) 432-6386

Training and Travel Programs

AZA Training Programs
Executive Office and Conservation Center
8304 Colesville Road
Silver Springs, Maryland 20910-3314
www.aza.org
(301) 907-7777

The various American Zoo and Aquarium Association (AZA)
schools are good training for anyone interested in a zoo or

aquarium career; however, most of the courses are open only to adults who are currently zoo professionals. The courses are generally one week in length and reasonably priced. The curriculum is solid and the courses also provide a great opportunity to meet and network with zoo and aquarium professionals.

Jersey Wildlife Preservation Trust
Les Augres Manor
Trinity, Jersey
Channel Islands JE3 5BP
Great Britain
011 44 1534 864 666
jerseyzoo@jwpt.org

Founded by legendary British conservationist and author Gerald Durrell, the Jersey program offers training in animal husbandry and conservation. This training center is one of the most renowned wildlife programs in the world.

NOLS (National Outdoor Leadership School)
288 Main Street
Lander, Wyoming 82520-3140
www.nols.edu
(307) 332-6973

NOLS, as the name implies, provides training in outdoor leadership. Offering outdoor programs for students age fifteen to ninety, NOLS uses the wilderness as a classroom in which to teach survival and respect for nature. Excellent programs for outdoor educators are also offered throughout the year. Most courses are two to four weeks in length, though some last a school semester.

Outward Bound
Route 9D
R2 Box 280
Garrison, New York 10524-9757
www.outwardbound.org
(1-800) 243-8520

Kurt Hahn founded Outward Bound in England in the 1930s with the motto "We are at our best when the way is steep." Outward Bound offers students of all ages challenging short-term programs of experiential education in the outdoors. I went on the thirty-one-day canoe trip through Quetico Provincial Park with Minnesota Outward Bound and I can attest that the program is valuable and life changing.

The School for Field Studies
16 Broadway
Beverly, Massachusetts 01915-4499
www.fieldstudies.org
(978) 927-7777

Offering credit for time spent in the field, the School for Field Studies gives college students a chance to break out of the classroom and head for the wild. Their catalog is a must read for those smitten by wanderlust.

Earthwatch
The Center for Field Research
680 Mt. Auburn Street
Box 9104
Watertown, Massachusetts 02272
www.earthwatch.org
(617) 926-8200

Earthwatch is one of those programs that works so well precisely because it is based upon a win-win scenario. Participants in an Earthwatch program generally spend from two weeks to a month assisting scientists with field research, both with their dollars and with their sweat and toil. This experience offers a hands-on approach to learning what the life of a field researcher is really like. Earthwatch programs are held all around the world and study everything from golden eagles on the coast of Scotland to the native people of New Guinea.

Peace Corps
1990 K Street, NW
Washington, D.C. 20526
www.peacecorps.gov
(1-800) 424-8580

Founded by President John F. Kennedy in 1963, the Peace Corps has provided the opportunity to work overseas for two generations of Americans. Peace Corps assignments vary, but today there are more wildlife- and environment-oriented opportunities than ever before. The Peace Corps is a great way to hone your language skills while helping to establish solid wildlife programs in a developing country.

Preparation

What are the three most important things you can do to prepare to work with wildlife?

READ, READ, READ!
What's the big deal about reading? Well first, books are the greatest human invention. Second, reading teaches you things about wildlife, expands what you know, and gives you time to think about what you're learning. Everyone I've ever met who is an expert on wildlife—from chimpanzee researcher Jane Goodall to David Rice, a third-grader from Mississippi who

So You Want to Work with Wildlife

Top 10 Things to Do	Top 10 Things NOT to Do
Be a sponge.	Have a parent call for you.
Become an expert on something.	Wait until you are an adult to get started.
Ask questions.	Hesitate because you are not already good at something.
Turn off your TV.	Worry about being "cool."
Spend time outside.	Think that individuals can't make a difference.
Learn a foreign language.	Worry about money.
Be curious.	Use the word *can't* a lot.
Read.	Think you already know it all.
Make yourself useful.	Show up late.
Have fun.	Whine and complain.

knows more about animals than most graduate biology students—started by reading. Experts are readers before they are experts.

Reading is a basic foundation of learning, so if you're not naturally drawn to books, maybe you're reading the wrong things. Find something you really want to learn about—something you think about all the time, like hawks, or pandas, or snakes. Read about that subject and I bet that soon you'll find yourself carrying around a book everywhere you go, just in case you get a minute to read. Remember, you can read in the car, or while waiting for someone, or before going to bed. Just soak it up.

Probably the best place to get started is with *National Geographic* magazine. We get many magazines that deal with nature at my house, but *National Geographic* is the best. It is well written, well researched, and, of course, has the best photos in the world.

FINDING YOUR NICHE

The world of work is like an ecosystem. As in nature, where every plant and animal has a niche, or a place in the system, each job that involves working with wildlife fills a particular niche. You need to find your place in the wildlife "system."

Here are some suggestions to guide you through the pressures of finding a job working with wildlife.

Look for a win-win relationship.
In nature this is called mutualism—when one organism helps another and they both benefit. With people, remember that cooperation isn't altruism, or selflessness.

Get a good compass.
Life is a journey, so it's important to have some idea of where you're headed. It is much easier to reach your goals if you are as clear as you can possibly be about where you want to go.

Get as much experience as possible.
Theory is not much good if it remains untested. Skills grow with experience. So be open to getting your foot in the door and starting at the bottom.

(continued)

Attitude is everything.

Jump in and show that you can get the job done. You don't need to be the smartest person in your organization. You'll get somewhere if you are the most enthusiastic and the hardest working.

Can't is a four-letter word.

If you don't believe in your dream, nobody else ever will either.

Never take no for an answer.

Most of the best ideas in wildlife conservation and biology were novel once and may even have been resisted at first. Keep going. As Garrison Keillor said, "The ship of hope often sinks nearly within sight of shore." So keep rowing!

Money is not the issue.

As Wendell Berry, the poet of Kentucky, put it, "The work of planet saving is humble work and will never make its effective pursuers wealthy." Forget about the money; focus on your goals.

Learn the language.

As in any field, there is a language unique to wildlife work. Behavioral ecologists use the most remarkable phrases to express the ideas of ethology, as do herpetologists in their work with reptiles. Whatever your specialty, if you're going to communicate with colleagues, you must know the language.

Incentive runs the world.

In a world of 6 billion people, relationships matter more than ever. Working closely with others makes it easier to move your projects forward, especially when everyone benefits.

A CLOSING REMINDER:
You Don't Have to Be a Rocket Scientist

If you want to work with wildlife, it doesn't really matter what field you ultimately choose. More often than not you will find full-time work, or find a way to volunteer for an organization that helps wildlife. So, if you want to be an accountant, think about being the zoo accountant. If you are interested in restaurant management, retailing, marketing, or public relations, look for a way to tie that career field to a wildlife activity. Conservation societies need public relations people. Zoos, natural history museums, and aquariums feed people and sell them things, and need people to provide these services. You don't have to take the "traditional" path of becoming someone who works directly with animals in order to have an impact.

It takes all of us working together to make a difference. Many people start down a traditional path and then realize that it's not what they really wanted. It doesn't mean that they no longer have an interest in wildlife, it just means they have found another career that is a better fit for them. So, I would suggest that the key is to find the career that fits your talents and interests. Once you have found that, then you can combine it with an interest in animals and make a positive difference for wildlife.

GLOSSARY

animal husbandry—the care and raising of animals in a zoo or aquarium, or domesticated animals on a farm or ranch

arboreal—adapted for living in trees

behaviorist—a scientist who studies the movements and behaviors of animals

biodiversity, biological diversity—the variety of all living things on Earth, as demonstrated by their genes, species, and ecosystems

biology—the area of science that studies plants and animals. The field of biology includes botany, ecology, and zoology.

botany—the study of plants

cryogenics—the science that deals with the production of very low temperatures. In relation to biology, cryogenics involves the freezing of living animal and plant tissue, often in liquid nitrogen.

chromosomes—the microscopic, threadlike bodies that carry the genes that convey inherited characteristics

DNA—*DeoxyriboNucleic Acid*, the molecule that carries the genetic code that gives living things their special characteristics

domesticated—animals and plants that have been bred to live with or be used by people

ecologist—a biologist who studies the interrelationships between living and nonliving things

ecosystem—a community of animals and plants, interacting with their environment

endangered—an animal or plant species at risk of extinction

endocrinologist—a scientist who studies the glands and hormones of animals

environmental education—educational programs relating to nature, the outdoors, and the ecological impact of altering the environment

ethnobotanist—a scientist who studies the uses of plants in relation to human culture

ethologist—a biologist who studies patterns of animal behavior under natural conditions

exotic animal—a wild, nondomesticated animal

field biologist—a scientist who conducts research outdoors in nature, rather than in a laboratory

genetic diversity—the variety of hereditary differences between plants and animals of the same species

geneticist—a scientist who specializes in the study of heredity and the relatedness of animals or plants of the same species

marine biology—the field of biological science focusing on the animals and plants of the ocean

nocturnal—active at night

nutritionist—a scientist who studies food and nourishment in relation to the animals that eat it

paleoanthropologist—a scientist who studies ancient human-like creatures

physiologist—a biologist who studies the parts and functions of living organisms

population management—human control of the numbers of a specific group of exotic animals or plants

primatologist—a scientist who studies the biology and behavior of monkeys, apes, and prosimians

satellite telemetry—the process of transmitting and collecting animal behavior data by way of satellite technology

scuba—scuba stands for *s*elf-*c*ontained *u*nderwater *b*reathing *a*pparatus. With scuba equipment, a person can swim underwater, breathing air from a tank strapped to the back and connected to the mouth by a hose

veterinarian—a doctor concerned with the medical and surgical treatment of animals

wildlife management—human organization and control of exotic animals living in a natural area

zoology—the field of the biological sciences that deals with the study of animals

FOR MORE INFORMATION

Books

Careers for Animal Lovers by Louise Miller, VGM Career Horizons, Lincolnwood, Ill, 1991.

The Complete Guide to Environmental Careers by Bill Sharp, Island Press, Washington, D.C., 1993.

They Work with Wildlife by Edward Ricciuti, Harper & Row, New York, 1983.

Internet Sources

Listed below are a sampling of websites that may help you explore the possibilities of working with wildlife. These will probably lead you to many other websites—some that deal with the general field, and some that take up specific topics.

Zoos and Aquariums

American Zoo and Aquarium Association *www.aza.org*
Bronx Zoo *www.wcs.org*
Cincinnati Zoo & Botanical Garden *www.cincyzoo.org*
Monterey Bay Aquarium *www.mbayaq.org*

Veterinary Medicine

DVM Magazine *www.dvmnewsmagazine.com/*
International Journal of
 Veterinary Medicine www.priory.com/vet.htm

Conservation Organizations

Conservation International *www.conservation.org*
National Audubon Society *www.audubon.org*
National Wildlife Federation *www.nwf.org*
The Nature Conservancy *www.tnc.org*
World Wildlife Fund *www.wwf.org*

Wildlife Awareness

American Museum of Natural History *www.amnh.org*
National Geographic Society *www.nationalgeographic.com*
The 90-Second Naturalist *www.nsnaturalist.org*

Wildlife and Conservation

http://planetpets.simplenet.com/wldorgs.htm
Global Rivers Environment Education Network
    www.igc.apc.org/green/
The Jane Goodall Institute *www.janegoodall.org*

Birds

Cornell Ornithology Lab *www.birds.cornell.edu*
American Birding Association *www.americanbirding.org*

Botany

Ethnobiology Conservation Team *www.ethnobotany.org*
Arizona Sonora Desert Museum *www.desertmuseum.org*

Ecotourism and Adventures

Outside Magazine *http://outside.starwave.com*
Outward Bound *www.outwardbound.org*
National Outdoor Leadership School *www.nols.org*

INDEX

Page numbers in *italics* indicate illustrations.